CLEAN UP
WITH
FRANCHISING

GLOBAL
PUBLISHING
G R O U P

Global Publishing Group
Australia • New Zealand • Singapore • America • London

DISCLAIMER

This publication contains general information, techniques, skills and concepts and should not be considered as personal advice. If a reader decides to use this information, they do so at their own discretion and the author and publishers do not assume any responsibility whatsoever under any condition or circumstance. It is advised that the reader seek their own independent advice.

Nothing in this book promises that you'll get the same results or in any way guarantees that what's worked for others is going to work for you.

In this book the author shares personal experiences building a commercial cleaning business and developing a franchise system. This book should in no way be considered an offer to sell a franchise. This book and the information contained in this book is for information purposes only, nor is it intended as an offer to sell a franchise or a solicitation of an offer to buy a franchise.

To avoid all doubt, if you're in the United States, the offering of a franchise can be made by prospectus only in the form of a Franchise Disclosure Document. In the states of California, Hawaii, Illinois, Indiana, Maryland, Michigan, Minnesota, New York, North Dakota, Oregon, Rhode Island, South Dakota, Virginia, Washington and Wisconsin you'll not be offered a franchise unless and until the applicable pre-sale registration and/or disclosure requirements have been complied with.

CLEAN UP
WITH
FRANCHISING

The Business Model for High Profits, Low Overheads, and Residual Income

DAMIEN BOEHM
International Author, Entrepreneur & Franchising Expert

First Edition 2023

National Library of Australia
Cataloguing-in-Publication entry:

Clean up with franchising: The Business Model for High Profits, Low Overheads, and Residual Income - Damien Boehm

1st ed.
ISBN: 978-1-925370-82-9 (pbk.)

 A catalogue record for this
book is available from the
National Library of Australia

Published by Global Publishing Group
PO Box 258, Banyo, QLD 4014 Australia
Email admin@globalpublishinggroup.com.au

For further information about orders:
Phone: +61 7 3267 0747

This book is dedicated to all the freedom-loving, free spirited entrepreneurs and aspiring entrepreneurs who are committed to making a positive difference to themselves, their families and the community they live and work in.

ACKNOWLEDGMENTS

I want to thank Bill Stack, Kirk Simpson and Brad Sugars for their support, invaluable insights, and relentless determination in helping Urban Clean achieve its success. Their contributions have been instrumental in our journey.

I also extend my appreciation to all our franchise partners who have joined us on this journey and contributed to some of our biggest breakthroughs as a business.

I am thankful to Sharon Jurd and John Sanders for their initial encouragement to write this book, and to Darren Stephens and Andrew Carter for their expert insights during the writing process.

Lastly, I express my profound gratitude to my wife Erikha for her unconditional love, unwavering support, and unyielding encouragement throughout the years. This book would not have been possible without her.

EXTRA BONUSES!!

EXTRA BONUSES HERE NOW!

We can't give you everything to get started in your business or franchise your business in one small book.

So we've created a very special website with loads of extra FREE resources, just for you.

You'll find interviews with experts, including some who were instrumental in building the Urban Clean system, covering the topics of this book.

There are checklists, reports, tips, and tools to help you start and grow your own business, invest in a franchise or become a franchisor.

Check out our Bonuses at:

www.CleanUpWithFranchising.com

TABLE OF CONTENTS

Introduction – Why this Book?   1

Chapter 1:   In Search of the Perfect Business   7

Chapter 2:   Disaster Strikes   15

Chapter 3:   Business Breakthrough   23

Chapter 4:   Why Commercial Cleaning?   35

Chapter 5:   Getting the Fundamentals Right   41

Chapter 6:   Getting Cleaning Contracts   49

Chapter 7:   Other Methods of Marketing   59

Chapter 8:   Even More Ways to Market Your Business   73

Chapter 9:   Keeping Business   81

Chapter 10:   Hiring Staff   91

Chapter 11:   Mistakes and Misconceptions   103

Chapter 12:   The Secret to Winning   115

Chapter 13:   Stages of a Janitorial Business   125

Chapter 14:   Franchising a Cleaning Business   131

Chapter 15:   Creating the Right Franchise Offer   141

Chapter 16:   Building Residual Income   149

Chapter 17:   A Unique Approach to Franchising   155

Afterword –   Call to Action   165

About Urban Clean   167

About The Author   170

INTRODUCTION – WHY THIS BOOK?

In 2011 I was broke, knocking on doors setting appointments for a roof restoration business.

Within a few short years I was collecting hundreds of thousands of dollars every month. This amount grew consistently every month, and that money came in whether I worked or not. My overheads were low. Cash flow was predictable. And bills were no longer a problem.

I'm not in banking, real estate, cryptocurrency or venture capital.

The industry I'm in is cleaning.

As I write this book in 2022, the world has been shaken by the COVID-19 pandemic. Cleaning is needed like never before. And over the coming years the industry will be going through a boom time. Now is the perfect time for you to be part of it.

The formula I uncovered and that I lay out in this book launched a global franchise.

This book is going to give you a step-by-step blueprint that I used to build a multimillion-dollar commercial cleaning business the fast and easy way. It's the same formula I've used to help other people build their very own six and seven figure businesses.

I'm no armchair expert either. I've been in the trenches. Starting with little more than a mop and a vacuum, I built a national multimillion-dollar business that's now growing internationally.

You are going to learn how to win cleaning account after cleaning account. I'm going to reveal what accounts you should be going for, how to win them and how to keep them, to grow a cleaning business predictably, profitably and fast.

I'll cover what traps you must look out for, what systems you must have in place, the stages all cleaning businesses go through and how to break through each stage to reach the next level.

I'll reveal how to get other people's money to finance the rapid growth of your business, how to create add-ons and cross-selling opportunities to generate multiple profit centers in your business.

You'll learn how you can use this model to become a franchisor yourself so you can rapidly expand your business without any of the headaches and frustrations that come from operating a traditional large cleaning business with the staff and the overheads that typically come with it.

The model in this book will show you how you can operate a cleaning empire without any employees and near zero overheads!

I stumbled into this business when everything seemed to be falling apart for me. I discovered a formula that unlocked the financial freedom I couldn't find anywhere else. I want to share my journey and this discovery with you. I want you to have the same financial security and time freedom that this business model has given me.

This is more than just a business to me. It's a mission.

You deserve to achieve financial independence. No one should be stuck in the rat race – including you. And there's no better way of achieving financial independence than by providing an honest, much needed service such as cleaning and helping others achieve their goals and provide for their families.

Lack and poverty are nobody's friends. Money might not buy happiness, but it will give you more choices, more experiences, and let you take care of the people you love.

I experienced poverty first hand growing up in Adelaide, Australia. I witnessed how it can push a family to breaking point. Money doesn't solve all problems, but it can solve a lot of them. What I do know is poverty can lead people to make desperate decisions that can hurt themselves and the people they love. Financial worry and stress benefit no one.

One of my earliest memories was sitting at the side of the road with my mum and sister watching smoke come out of the old black Morris Minor that had broken down once again. My mum sobbed uncontrollably as the tow-truck carried it away for the last time. Our cars were always breaking down. We had lodgers so we could cover the rent. My mum worked long hours as a nurse to just pay the bills. There was never enough money.

We were poor. Others always had more than us. As a child I just accepted it. I knew I had less than other kids. I didn't like it, but it was our reality. It was normal to me.

It's strange that as a kid I seemed most upset about my school uniform. I was the kid that wore the school uniform that didn't quite fit because I had to have whatever was left in the remainder bin.

Life took a dramatic turn for me at 15. The pressure of being a single mum finally got too much for my mum. She left to move interstate by herself. My sister ran away and lived on the streets before being placed in foster care. I dropped out of school.

I wasn't left destitute, though. I had a house to live in. I still had to cover my food, travel and clothing expenses but having a place to live kept me off the streets. I survived off less than $50 a week for over a year before finding proper work. Even in the mid-90s that wasn't a lot of money in Australia. I was just happy to avoid foster care. Some days were easier than others. I recall walking home hungry one night. It was raining. I was desperate for food, and prayed. My eyes turned downward to the gutter, and there on the ground was a $2 coin! I have never been so happy to come across money! I went to the shop to buy a bag of potatoes – don't ask me why potatoes – it was something $2 could buy and something I knew how to cook.

I started going to the library and I discovered a love of books. This love of learning got me back into school and eventually university.

On graduating I traveled throughout Asia, worked as an English teacher, returned to Australia, got married and started my own family.

There was no way I was going to let my family go through what I did growing up. After a couple of small ventures, I set my sights on real estate as the vehicle to provide financial security for my family.

In the ensuing chapters I'm going to share with you how that went and how cleaning ended up as the unlikely solution I was always looking for.

I'll share my story, my mistakes and breakthroughs.

By the end of this book you'll have a recipe for building residual income in one of the most stable recession proof businesses there is.

There's a good chance you picked up this book because you're looking at getting started in a new venture, you're interested in franchising, curious about getting started in a commercial cleaning business or you've already got a cleaning business and you're stuck and want to take it to the next level.

If so, you've picked the right book.

In the pages of this book, I'm going to share with you how I cracked the code to winning as many cleaning contracts as I could possibly handle. I'm also going to reveal the three essential elements you've got to get right if you want to succeed in this business.

This book doesn't just cover cleaning. It shows how the franchising model can be used to give you a huge head start in business if you're new to the industry and how it can provide massive leverage as a franchisor if you're looking at rapidly expanding a cleaning business with minimal overheads.

What I don't cover in this book is the nuts and bolts and set up requirements of a commercial cleaning business, such as company structure, insurances, equipment or for that matter even detailed cleaning methodologies.

This book won't show you how to clean. There are plenty of other books that will go through the basic requirements of setting up a business and how to clean. And of course, this training is available for everyone who joins a franchise system such as Urban Clean.

This book is about the business side of cleaning. It's about what it takes to create and manage a large cleaning business. It's about how to build a 6-figure commercial cleaning business in your spare time and turn it into a high 6 figure and 7 figure business or more.

It's a topic I'm deeply passionate about. I've obsessed about commercial cleaning for years – how to win contracts, how to keep them, how to build, train and motivate teams. This obsession led me to build a commercial cleaning franchise that's helped hundreds escape the rat race and become their own boss.

It certainly wasn't always like that. I made slow progress in the beginning and made many mistakes. I'll share my mistakes so you don't have to repeat them yourself.

This book doesn't promise a get-rich-quick formula. It will require work and consistency. If you're looking at building a seven-figure business that adds significant new revenue every year, it's going to require consistent application of hard work following a proven method. Even if you're looking at a smaller business with revenues of only a couple hundred thousand a year, it's going to require work.

If you just want to press a button, lie on the couch and watch the money roll in, this is the wrong book. You must apply it and work at it.

But what I write about has worked for me, and I've personally helped hundreds of people achieve their goals with a cleaning business.

If this book makes sense to you, and you're serious about taking the next step, I invite you to be one of them.

But enough of the intro, let's get started.

CHAPTER 1:
In Search of the Perfect Business

CHAPTER 1:
IN SEARCH OF THE PERFECT BUSINESS

"Would you tell me, please, which way I ought to go from here?"

"That depends a good deal on where you want to get to," said the Cat.

"I don't much care where," said Alice.

"Then it doesn't matter which way you go," said the Cat.

Alice's Adventures in Wonderland: Lewis Carroll

The Goal of Business Ownership

Before we cover how to build and grow a commercial business, we want to stop for a moment to consider what we want to get out of a business.

Why do we want to get into business in the first place? Where do we want to get to with a business venture?

The real reason to get into business is not to do what a business does, whether that be accounting, landscaping, preparing food, making coffees or cleaning. What matters is what a business gets you and the impact you make doing it.

When I conduct workshops and ask groups what they want out of owning a business their list normally includes:

- Freedom
- More time
- Flexibility
- Control
- Being in charge of their future and destiny
- Being their own boss
- More money
- Spending more time with their family
- Not missing out on their kids' childhood
- Having time and money to pursue their passions and hobbies
- Making a difference
- Not pinching pennies

Did you notice this list doesn't mention doing more of what a business does to make money? It doesn't matter what a business does if it lets you do more of what matters to you, whether that be spending time with family, leaving a legacy, donating to charity, or living your dream lifestyle.

Once you're clear on what you want out of a business, it's going to be easier to choose or design the right business for you.

Clarity is power.

When I first set out in business, making money was enough for me. I didn't pay much attention to how much time or risk I took on in pursuit of it. After starting a family, I realized I didn't want to be working all hours of the day or taking big gambles that could risk everything we had. I wasn't willing to miss out on my kids' childhood just to make money. I didn't want to trade dollars for hours.

I wanted a business that would give me more time, more money, more freedom. It had to be a business that could work without me.

And owning a business is without doubt one of the surest ways of creating wealth and time flexibility.

Of the 2755 billionaires listed on the Forbes Rich List, over 71% of them are self-made and 93% of their wealth had been created from business.

Business ownership is not risk free. There are plenty of mistakes you can make when starting and buying a business. I see people making five key mistakes when starting out and choosing a business for themselves.

Mistake #1: Thinking you must own a business in an industry you're passionate about or have experience in.

This might be a strange one to mention considering how often you see inspirational quotes telling you to follow your passion. A survey conducted by CB Insights showed that the three biggest causes of 92% startup failures were due to running out of funds, offering a service or product that nobody wants and having a poor business model. Only 5% of startups failed because they got burnt out or lost passion for the business. Again, what industry you're in, and what the business does is much less important than getting the results you want out of the business. And you're only going to get those results by understanding market fundamentals and having a business model that will deliver you the lifestyle you want.

Mistake #2: When assessing opportunities, not understanding how breakeven relates to business risk.

A business reaches breakeven when sales cover costs. Not all costs are the same. There are what are called fixed costs and variable costs. Fixed costs are costs you have no matter what sales you make. They are things such as rent, vehicles, employees, rates, internet, phone and software. Variable costs only happen when a sale is made. Sometimes variable costs are called costs of goods sold or COGS. When you make a sale, the revenue you receive minus your variable cost to sell that item is what's called your gross profit or contribution margin. The most important financial numbers in a business are fixed costs and contribution margin. The smaller your fixed costs are and the higher your contribution margin, the less risk and the more profitable a business is going to be.

For example, if you had a coffee shop, you might work out that your fixed costs everyday are $500. This is the cost just to open up for the day. It would include costs like your rent, equipment costs, wages and electricity.

To just break even and cover costs you need to make $500 in gross profit every day.

Let's say you sell a cup of coffee for $5. It costs you $1 of ingredients in coffee beans, milk and sugar to make a cup. So, $5 minus $1, gives you a $4 contribution margin per cup of coffee sold. This means you would need to sell 125 cups of coffee to reach breakeven and start making money.

You might find after doing a little research that your coffee shop location could reasonably only sell 100 cups a day. That sounds like a decent number but you're going to go broke if that's all you sell. You'll be losing $100 a day or $3000 a month.

If you want to avoid this risk, choose a business that has low fixed costs.

Mistake #3: Not recognizing the importance of recurring revenue.

Having recurring revenue is the reverse of fixed costs. Fixed costs are costs you know you have whether you make sales or not. Recurring revenue is cash flow and profits you know you have regardless of whether you make a sale or not.

Recurring revenue is even better when it's contractual and customers are happy to sign multiyear contracts.

What's even better than recurring revenue is compounding revenue. This happens when you can add recurring revenue clients without reaching market saturation or operational capacity. I'll talk about this in more detail in a later chapter on commercial cleaning contracts.

Mistake #4: Thinking you've got to get into an industry that doesn't have a lot of competition.

Competition is a sign that there's a market for what you've got. Shark feeding frenzies happen where there are many fish.

Competition can have a negative impact on prices but only if you don't differentiate your service from others and or have any unique point of difference. In a later chapter I'll share how I did this for a cleaning service.

Competition is even better when the industry is huge and fragmented with no single player taking more than 20% market share. This means there is plenty of opportunity for everyone, especially local business operators.

Mistake #5: Thinking you've got to work it out on your own.

As entrepreneurs we like to do things all on our own. We have a 'can-do' attitude. And this gets us far. Sometimes it slows us down. Do you really want to repeat someone else's ten years of trial and error, mistakes and dead ends, just so you can say you did it all yourself?

Successful people model other people's success. If someone's already done it, there's no need to reinvent the wheel.

I've invested hundreds of thousands of dollars learning from others and at the start of my journey I was actively looking for a franchise because I saw no point reinventing a system if someone had already created it.

PRO TIP

Look out for 5 things in a business:

Marketability - Does the business sell something everybody already wants and needs?

Market Size - Is the market huge or small? 1% of a multibillion-dollar market is better than 20% of a one-million-dollar market.

Recurring Revenue Model - Do customers have to keep buying what you've got, and will they sign contracts to buy your product or service?

Employment Market - Do you have to get a highly skilled and specialized workforce or can most people with the right training and attitude do the work?

Lifestyle - Will the business achieve your personal and lifestyle goals?

I'm sharing these mistakes because I've made all of them. I've had businesses that relied on constant sales to stay afloat each month. I've not understood breakeven and suffered with cash flow. I've started businesses that had little competition, later to find no one wanted the service I was providing.

The business I was looking for had to be low risk, have high returns, give me time and flexibility for myself and it had to be a business that could operate without me.

I wanted a business that had the following.

- A huge market with a product or service that was always in demand
- A business that could operate without me and allow me to take holidays even from the get-go
- Low upfront investment
- Home based or low rent
- Low equipment costs
- Low employment costs and staff management
- Compounding contractual income
- Fully systemized, with proven methods for sales and operations
- Low stock and inventory management
- Opportunity to make high ticket sales
- Low overheads
- High average profits without multiple locations
- Recurring, residual or subscription-based income

And lastly a business that could allow me to have a multi-million-dollar business without a single employee.

I wanted a business that gave me TIME, MONEY & FREEDOM.

I went looking for one and I couldn't find one. So, I made one.

The ensuing chapters share that journey.

CHAPTER 2:
Disaster Strikes

CHAPTER 2:
DISASTER STRIKES

"Every adversity, every failure, every heartbreak, carries with it the seed of an equal or greater benefit." – *Napoleon Hill*

"Here's a $500 deposit, and we'll pay the rest in two weeks."

I had just put an ad in the paper to sell my small commercial cleaning business. And I had a buyer.

It was 2010 and my property development business was doing great. Or so I thought. I had just completed a small unit project and banked a cool $400,000 ready to put in the next project. The small cleaning business that I had on the side seemed nothing more than a distraction. Why keep this thing, I thought. I was on a roll. The cleaning business was paying me pocket change compared to my property business. So, I put it up for sale and it wasn't long before I had someone ready to buy.

I had started a commercial cleaning business about a year prior to solve my cash flow problems.

I had done this before. I had previously built and sold off a cleaning business. In just a few short months I built a cleaning round and I sold it for nearly more money than I made during the time I had the business. So, I knew there was money in cleaning.

I wanted a side business because I was living project to project. I went from one consulting job to another and one property development to the next. Cash was haphazard and erratic. What I lacked was consistent regular income. A cleaning business and in particular a commercial cleaning business promised regular, stable, recession-proof income. So,

I started one on the side. Somehow by sheer luck I picked up a handful of clients. But I was barely scraping in $50,000 a year with it.

It wasn't a big focus of mine. My focus was my property business. After some years learning the ropes and working for others in property development, I went out on my own and developed small inner-city parcels of land into units and townhouses.

I was happy with my property business, and was glad to sell my cleaning business.

Then I got a call a week later from the buyer.

"I'm sorry, we can't go through with the sale. You can keep the deposit."

The sale of my cleaning business fell through.

And it was just as well it did.

Less than twelve months later, I had no real estate projects and was looking for a job.

PRO TIP

Be careful getting drawn into businesses or lifestyles that seem sexy and glamorous.

Ego doesn't pay the bills. It's easy to overlook businesses that seem boring and unglamorous, but the truth is there's nothing sexier in business than profit and returns.

In January 2011, South East Queensland, Australia, experienced one of its biggest floods in history. An inland tsunami washed through the center of the city of Toowoomba. Half of Brisbane's Central Business District was underwater. Sharks swam down Ipswich's main street. Brisbane residents were using kayaks to get in and out of their homes.

The six months leading up to the flood, it rained non-stop nearly every day. It was so wet that the streets of Brisbane had clumps of green algae growing in the gutters because of the never-ending stream of water.

I had three development sites in progress at the time. It rained. Then it rained some more. One of my development sites resembled the muddy swamp in front of Yoda's hut. Construction was delayed. Costs blew out. My business partners' building company went into liquidation. The market dropped, and people who had placed deposits on my units were pulling out of their sale contracts. To top it all off, a Development Application that I had lodged in council for one of my projects was rejected.

The bank called a meeting. With the market dropping, my business partner going into liquidation, I was given a choice to put more money in and take over the loans or sell. My cash reserves weren't enough, and I didn't have enough cash flow to cover all the debt on my own.

I was forced to sell everything at a loss.

Rule 1: Cash flow before capital gains.

Cash flow is always king. Cash flow gives you options. The more consistent and secure that cash flow is, the more valuable it is. Think of how banks lend. They look first at income and cash flow then how much you contribute in terms of capital. Your capital outlay only lowers their risk in case of a worst-case scenario. Serviceability matters more to a lender than capital. A lack of strong cash flow put me in a very vulnerable position that severely limited my options.

I was devastated.

I was also broke.

I got a job during the day setting appointments for a roof restoration company.

In the evening, I went out and cleaned the handful of clients I had with the cleaning business I started on the side.

It was a humble time for me. From having millions of dollars in assets, I was now just making ends meet, knocking on doors during the day and vacuuming floors at night. But I was grateful for it. It was a time that allowed me to focus on family, my spirituality, and the things most important to me.

This was my life for some two years. I was making a living, but it certainly wasn't the life I had envisioned for myself or my family.

One day I woke up and realized that this life would be the rest of my life UNLESS I made a decision and took action.

So, I made a decision.

All I had at the time was this small commercial cleaning business I had started on the side. I made a commitment to making it work.

If this business was going to work for me, I had to build a consistent recurring income by securing commercial cleaning contracts. Winning those contracts couldn't cost me a lot of money and business growth had to be self-funding. And ultimately it had to be a business that could work without me.

I invested what little spare funds I had into business coaching.

I hustled. I did whatever I could to win contracts. I got referrals. I advertised online. I did direct marketing drops and knocked on doors.

I started to make progress. It was slow at first. But I started to gain traction. I would do a good job and get a referral for more work. I experimented relentlessly, learnt everything I could about the commercial cleaning industry, everything I could about managing cleaning staff and everything I could about marketing and selling a cleaning service. Slowly but surely, I was growing my business.

I then experienced my first real lesson in the commercial cleaning industry. One of my accounts was a growing finance company. I landed the account when their office premises were relatively small. When I started cleaning for them it was a three times weekly account, and billing was less than $3000 per month. There were about 50 desks in the office.

They were growing rapidly. So much so that they had to relocate to a new office about three times the size. They loved my service, so they asked me to quote a daily cleaning service for the new office. I quoted at $90,000 a year and was awarded the contract. I took pride in providing a premium service, and asked a premium price for this service.

All went well for a while. It was the gem in my cleaning portfolio. Then one day I got a call from someone out of the blue.

"Hi, is this Damien Boehm, of Urban Clean?"

"Yes"

"My name is Michael from XYZ Cost Cutting Consultancy, I've been appointed by Fast Growing Finance Company [if you didn't already guess that's not their real names] to review a number of services including cleaning. We're inviting two other cleaning companies to tender. They're happy with your level of service, so you're invited to be part of the tender and resubmit a quote."

"OK. This is all news to me. Happy to work with you, but I'd like to speak first with Fast Growing Finance Company."

"Actually, they've requested on my recommendation that you only speak with me during the tender process. I'll send you an email shortly with my authorization form and what I require from you to submit a proposal."

I was given two weeks to submit the tender. I had never worked so hard on a proposal. I showed all the systems I had to ensure the cleaning was always done to a high standard. I showed all the workings I used to calculate my price.

It was all in vain.

The other quotes were nearly half my price. The cost consultant had handpicked the other cleaning companies knowing they would submit low-ball prices.

The account was given to one of the other bidders.

I was given an opportunity to ask for feedback. So, I asked.

The Cost Consultant's response was an eye-opener.

"To be blunt, you're far too expensive. Your pricing was uncompetitive and, being so much more than the other quotes, you lost all credibility. I saw your calculations. Asking for 20% or more in profit for cleaning is near ridiculous. After all, you guys are really just in the labor hire business. With the money they're going to save, they could bring on another junior or assistant if they wanted."

It hurt too. This account was a fair chunk of my business at the time.

It turned out this client's stock price had dropped, and they were looking at all ways to reduce expenditure in the company that was not core to their operations.

Having one client make up more than 10% of your business makes your business vulnerable. I sweated over this account. And it hurt when I lost it. I vowed never again to sweat over any single one client.

Rule 2: Never make one client make up more than 10% of your business.

Larger accounts have greater price sensitivity. It did not matter that the Fast Growing Finance Company had the money to pay extra for the cleaning. Their annual revenue was well in excess of $20 million. They definitely had the money. What mattered was what they could do with the extra money saved by using a cheaper supplier. When this amount is not large, it's not a big factor in their decision-making process. When it's close to or equal to someone's salary then it gets attention.

I was reminded of this point some years later when I was invited by a school to put a tender in for the cleaning. This was a large school. I don't chase this work because I know how cut-throat and price sensitive it is. But it was a referral and I agreed to put a bid in. My price was $1,070,000 per year. I squeezed the numbers and studied efficiencies to make my price competitive. There was going to be no dawdling on this site. The cleaners were going to have to move and be productive. We worked out the perfect routing, what machines and tools were to be used to cut down time and do the perfect job. Everything was timed to the minute. It was tighter than two coats of paint. I allowed only for a 10% margin. And I knew that was optimistic. Another company won with a bid that was less than $900,000 a year. Assuming that the cleaning company was paying correct salaries and allowances to their cleaners, I can only guess how barebones their cleaning schedule would have had to be and how tight their margins were.

But I understand the school's perspective. If they were confident the other cleaning company would do a reasonable job, why spend an additional $170,000 a year. That money could pay for at least two extra full-time teachers or a new science lab.

Rule 3: The bigger the account, the smaller the profit.

The bigger the account the more downward pressure there is on price. Once an account is more than someone's full-time salary, there will be greater scrutiny on the price.

This is especially the case when the cleaning bill is a significant expense item for a business. When reducing the cleaning bill will have a noticeable impact on a company's bottom line profits, it's guaranteed to get the attention of management.

Losing this account made me relook at all my accounts.

CHAPTER 3:
Business Breakthrough

CHAPTER 3:
BUSINESS BREAKTHROUGH

"The secret to success is to do the common things uncommonly well." –
John D. Rockefeller

As much as it hurt at the time, losing a key account was one of the best things that could have happened to me at that time. It made me reevaluate all the business I had.

Some of my accounts were great. They were easy to work with, profitable, loyal, and paid on time.

I wanted more just like them.

Others were difficult to work with, refused to give after-hours access, were slow to pay and barely profitable.

So, I graded my customers into 'A', 'B', 'C', and 'D' customers. 'A' customers were my best. 'D' customers were my worst.

I ranked customers according to level of gross income, how easy they were to work with, how loyal and secure the account was, gross margin, and whether they were good payers.

'A' customers were accounts over $2000 per month, they were a pleasure to do business with, gave afterhours access, were loyal, were never going to look elsewhere if I continued to provide a good service, gross margin was in excess of 40%, and they always paid on time.

'D' customers were accounts less than $500 per month, painful to work with, made unreasonable requests, everything was a problem, didn't give afterhours access, treated my service as a commodity, were always looking for the cheapest service, gross margin was barely single digits, and they were always late and delinquent in payment.

I decided to let go of my 'D' customers. I gave them plenty of notice to get new cleaners. I figured they cost me money and were never going to bring referrals. Even if they were to bring referrals, if they referred clients just like them, I wouldn't want them anyway.

My 'C' grade customers had to become 'B' or 'A' grade customers, otherwise I had to let them go too. The easiest way to do this was to make a friendly call and inform them I was going to raise my prices or in the case of non-payers stop service. Some of them said yes. Others said no. I was okay either way.

At first, I couldn't believe I was doing this. It was counterintuitive to everything I believed about business. After all, I had chased their business at some point. Was I really going to let go of them, and tell them to go elsewhere?

I did not enjoy making these calls, but it was such a relief to do this. It felt like a load had dropped from my shoulders. I could now concentrate on my "A" and "B" customers.

Rule 4: Not all dollars are made equal. A dollar is not a dollar in business. Some customers are not worth chasing and will cost you dearly if you pursue them.

My attention was now turned to my 'A' customers. The big question was how was I going to get more of them.

First, I looked at what they had in common.

Cleaning was important to them. They were principally medical centers and professional offices, where appearance and hygiene mattered.

Cleaning was not a significant cost to their business. Whether they spent an extra few hundred dollars or even a thousand or two in some cases, made little difference to them.

And it made sense. A legal practice with 20 staff would be paying close to $2 million a year in salaries alone. Their cleaning bill might not be much more than $25,000 a year. Yet if potential clients walked into a dirty, smelly, messy office, they could be losing hundreds of thousands, even millions of dollars of potential business. The legal principal doesn't want her staff either to lose productivity because they need to chase up the cleaners for things they should have done, or worse still, get their lawyers taking out trash because their cleaners forgot to. Clients like this I found were happy to pay extra.

Rule 5: Clients will pay more when outcomes are important, and budgets are flexible.

These were the customers I wanted. And I wanted lots of them. Trouble was, so did a hundred other cleaning companies.

The challenge I faced was how I was going to stand out from every other cleaning service. I promised a great clean and had references and testimonials. But so did everyone else. I tried making changes to my service offering. I offered free cleans. I added extras to my service. Nothing was really sticking.

Then I had what I've since learnt to call a 'blinding flash of the obvious'. Instead of trying to guess what my ideal client wanted, I just asked them.

I had already identified who my 'A' grade clients were. It only made sense that what my existing 'A' grade clients wanted from a cleaning service, would be the same or similar to what other potential clients just like them wanted.

So I asked all my 'A' grade clients what an ideal cleaning service looked like to them.

I interviewed each of them, asked questions, listened and took notes.

I looked at all their responses and noticed six common points that came up again and again.

These six points were

- Specific Cleaning Outcomes
- Consistency
- Communication
- Transparency
- Security
- Professional Partnership

First was Specific Cleaning Outcomes. Most offices had specific things unique to them they wanted cleaned every single time. If that one thing was missed, it didn't matter how well the rest of the cleaning was carried out, as far as that office was concerned the cleaning hadn't been done.

I remember once quoting an office that looked like it was getting serviced well. The front glass and front reception area were clean and even smelt fresh. After being shown the office and the requirements of the cleaning scope, I asked, "Why are you looking at changing cleaners?" The office manager replied, "Do you see that windowsill in the corner of my office? At morning tea, I like to sit over there and look out the window. It bugs me to see any dust on the windowsill. I've mentioned it a few times to the cleaners but they only occasionally get it done." As far as that office manager was concerned if that windowsill was not dusted, the rest of the clean was irrelevant.

For each office, those specific items will be different. Sometimes it's the sinks that are important. Sometimes it's an odor. Other places it can be topping up consumables or it's the hallway to the CEO's office. There are usually one or two things that absolutely have to be taken care of, for that office to feel they're being serviced well.

My ideal client wanted me to find out from them what specific things mattered to them and take care of them every clean.

Between 2020 and 2022, the most important outcome for the majority of clients was a safe, hygienic workplace. They wanted peace of mind, knowing surfaces had been properly cleaned and disinfected. They also wanted to prove to staff, customers and stakeholders that the cleaning and disinfection was happening to an objective and demonstrable standard. We did this by using a luminometer to test adenosine triphosphate (ATP) residual on surfaces after we cleaned them. This is the same process used in hospital environments to report on cleaning standards.

Consistency was second. It almost goes without saying customers want a reliable, consistent service, executed to the same high standard each and every time.

It seems like such a basic requirement, but for a cleaning company to deliver this requires significant planning, preparation, training and systems. It doesn't happen by accident.

The reason consistency is haphazard at best in the cleaning industry is that standards and systems are left to the individual ability and care of each cleaner. A good, conscientious cleaner will lock doors, check everything, clean well and double check to make sure they miss nothing. A bad cleaner will leave doors unlocked, miss items and clean poorly. A poorly trained cleaner will rush, miss things and be unsystematic in their approach to cleaning.

When cleaning standards and systems are left to cleaners it's no wonder consistency is hit and miss. Left to themselves, each cleaner will do things differently. They will have different cleaning standards. They will have different ways of communicating. Some will be more conscientious than others.

Consistency is the responsibility of the cleaning company. It's the cleaning company's job to create systems of uniformity, to set the standards of what is clean and what's not, to train all the cleaners to follow the same process and procedures. This ensures consistency.

Clients don't want surprises. They expect the same standard of service every time.

Communication too was a constant point of frustration for businesses dealing with their cleaners. Office managers had no idea who they were supposed to communicate with or send messages to.

Cleaners may not be native speakers either so don't understand simple instructions. And when supervisors and operation managers get involved messages directly to the cleaners can get misinterpreted or not relayed correctly.

Transparency was critical in winning their trust. Because commercial cleaning happens mainly at night, cleaning companies sometimes think they can get away with just about anything. Cleaning might be rushed through. Untrained, un-inducted staff could turn up. Keys are given to friends who are paid in cash to do the job.

Clients want transparency. They want to know who turns up, what they do, when they do it and that cleaning staff are getting paid correctly.

Security was critical to these businesses as well. No one wants to hand keys to criminals. Clients wanted to know how cleaners were screened and vetted. A police check is the very minimum.

Clients want confidence in the opening and closing procedures of a cleaning business. They wanted to know that in the case of lost keys there's nothing identifiable on them.

Cleaners have unparalleled access to offices and workplaces after hours. Clients wanted to know that there is a strict rule of confidentiality practiced by a cleaning company.

If there wasn't a confidentiality agreement in place, there may be ambiguity among cleaning staff about what can or cannot be discussed or looked at. A business might be at risk of having confidential information inadvertently divulged.

It is expected that a professional cleaning company would make it very clear that anything seen or heard at a client's premises was strictly confidential and should not be shared with anyone.

Lastly, clients are looking for a professional partnership with their cleaners. The reason a business chooses to engage a cleaning business is because they want to outsource the upkeep and maintenance of their workplace. And they don't want to manage it either.

They don't want me to wait for them to tell me what needed to be done. They want me to make suggestions and solve their problems as a professional. It's your role to make recommendations on the frequency of the clean and one-off jobs.

PRO TIP

Often the answer to your problems is right in front of you.

We can spend so much time trying to work out what our customers want and how to create an amazing experience for them. Sometimes all it takes is just to ask them what they want.

The thing that surprised me the most was that price was not on the list. Many of them told me that if they were sure of getting what they wanted from a cleaning service, they would happily pay extra.

My ideal clients had just revealed to me what they wanted. It was now my job to spell out what those wants meant.

So, I went about designing simple solutions around those needs.

I asked myself what the simplest way was to ensure specific cleaning outcomes were achieved for each client. What training, systems, and auditing could I put in place to ensure a consistent standard of cleaning? I repeated this process for transparency, communication, security and professional relationships.

I created a mobile app, designed clear communication methods, simplified training, set clear standards and most importantly designed a client-centric business model that provided full transparency.

It seemed to me, the cleaning industry had created norms that were outdated and suited cleaning companies first and foremost, not the client. There was an obsession around rigid adherence to cleaning scopes. Subcontracting was a widespread and common practice. They were not sure ultimately who was going to end up cleaning their premises after they signed a contract. Clients had come to accept this as a norm. They didn't like it but had resigned themselves to it.

The effect of these changes was immediate. I saw an immediate jump in my sales conversions. People started telling me that this was the service they were always looking for but could never find.

I started to win contract after contract.

This became a problem for me.

Most of my business at the time was centrally located around the Brisbane CBD. I started to win contracts all over Brisbane and beyond.

The problem lay with my method of marketing. My marketing at that point was mainly digital. I was using paid search ads, online lead platforms, SEO and some telemarketing. This meant my contracts were scattered over a wide geographic area. This kind of marketing meant I had to cast a wide net to get enough lead volume.

I could have limped along slowly with very few leads located in a small geographic area or relied on referrals. But I wanted to grow fast. I wanted lots of leads.

Don't worry, there is another way of building a client portfolio quickly that ensures your clients are located close to each other. And best of all, this method allows you to take advantage of the most profitable segment of the market. I just didn't know that method at the time. In a later chapter, I'll show you how to avoid this when building your client portfolio.

The result, at this stage in my business, was I was winning contracts sometimes separated by 30 minutes to an hour from each other. During this time I had started a small number of cleaning contracts in Capalaba which was about an hour's drive from the center of Brisbane. The total value of these contracts was not much more than $3000 per month. My cleaners didn't like driving out there to do one or two small jobs, and it didn't make sense to pay for the travel time, so I decided to put these contracts up for sale.

I listed them on an online classified site called Gumtree, and the phone didn't stop ringing.

I was amazed that so many people were interested in purchasing these contracts. I wasn't giving these contracts away either. My asking price was over $15,000.

Cleaning Contracts are Assets

I learnt that cleaning contracts were valuable commodities. They trade like cars and real estate.

What was clear though when I spoke to people on the phone was that hardly any of them had a clue how to operate a commercial cleaning business.

They wanted contracts so they could earn extra income after hours and thought cleaning was simple and straightforward – something just about anyone can do. Some of them had a cleaning business already but had no idea how to win contracts on their own.

I was afraid that if I sold these contracts to them, they would lose the accounts after a few months. It was also clear they needed much more than a little guidance. They needed systems, support, coaching and mentoring.

And that's when the penny dropped.

I discovered there was a huge number of people looking for an afterhours commercial cleaning business, but needed guidance and support to retain business and grow it. And the market was big.

So, I franchised the business.

It was slow at first. In the first year we recruited just five franchisees but it quickly accelerated. In the second year we recruited and set up over 20 and we've continued to grow ever since.

There were other commercial cleaning franchises, of course. I was not the first to discover this market. I even remember when I first got started in commercial cleaning, I explored commercial cleaning franchises. The reason I chose not to invest in one was not because of the initial investment or ongoing fees. It was the lack of opportunity. All the franchises I had investigated provided contracts and initial training, but I wanted to grow my business. I wanted to learn. It was made quite clear to me that I was essentially subcontracting or buying a job in the evenings. I wanted more. I wanted them to teach me how to win contracts, grow my business, and develop teams of cleaners. None of them offered this.

When it was my turn to franchise, I wanted to offer people a real business opportunity not a job.

I wanted franchise partners that were in it to be business owners, not cleaners. I saw how easy it was to build a business past six and even seven figures. I wanted to give others the same opportunity. It was just a matter of getting some fundamentals right and following a system that worked.

I documented and systematized my entire business. The processes and steps I created to win commercial cleaning contracts, run the business and manage cleaning teams were made available to every franchisee. After years of investment, trial and error and obsessing about commercial cleaning and commercial cleaning franchising, I created franchise, master franchise and license opportunities for anyone wanting to fast track their way to success in commercial cleaning.

In a later chapter, I'll share exactly how I went about franchising the business and the method I used to recruit over one hundred franchise partners.

When franchising is done right everybody wins. Franchisees get to fast track their growth using a proven repeatable model. They get ongoing support as they grow their business. They're set up in business and then shown how to expand and grow it.

I'm proud to have helped many people get their business into multiple six and seven figures.

CHAPTER 4:
Why Commercial Cleaning?

CHAPTER 4:
WHY COMMERCIAL CLEANING?

"Success isn't always about greatness. It's about consistency. Consistent hard work leads to success. Greatness will come." – Dwayne Johnson

So why cleaning, of all things?

Let's be honest, It's not sexy or prestigious. And you're definitely not going to impress anyone when you tell them you own a cleaning business.

It's simple really.

Businesses need commercial cleaners. It's not trendy. It's boring, stable, lucrative and future proof.

I understood this intuitively when I decided to start a commercial cleaning business. It wasn't until I started growing a cleaning business that I saw the power in the numbers.

You see, cleaning is not optional for businesses. There's no surer way for a business to lose credibility than to have dirty, unhygienic premises. If winning and retaining clients, customers, and patrons matters to a business, cleaning will be a priority. If staff morale matters, cleaning will be a priority. No one argues this. This is great news for you. Most businesses have already budgeted for it. And especially with the advent of COVID-19, businesses have never been more sensitive to hygiene and cleanliness.

You don't need to convince any business they need cleaning.

Any business with more than five staff is going to need a cleaning service. And contrary to what many people think or say, even in the cleaning industry, if you know what market to target and how to meet that target's needs, you DON'T need to compete on price.

There are lots of things I like about this industry.

You have the ability to make a real, tangible difference to the appearance of a business. You can increase staff morale and make a positive difference to people's days. It's an honest business – call me weird but there's real satisfaction knowing you're making toilets clean and carpets spotless. It's dirty work and sometimes unappreciated but you know what you do is needed and critical to the healthy function of an office.

It's a deceptively simple business too. Which is why there's so much opportunity in it. I say deceptively simple because cleaning tasks themselves are generally easy and straightforward. Anyone with basic training can perform them. However, delivering on them well, according to client requirements and needs, and creating systems to do that time and time again – that's a challenge few have mastered and achieved. Many people who try entering the market thinking that all that's required is a website and cleaning gear, get a rude shock.

There's never a problem finding people to clean. There's also never a problem finding a buyer for cleaning contracts. They're a hot commodity. Which gives your business lots of options if you know how to win contracts. I'll cover these options later in the book.

Your clients sign contracts with you too. This gives you income security. Residential clients won't sign contracts and will dispense with your service as soon as it's convenient for them. They go on holiday, service is paused. A partner loses a job or stays at home, that's the end of the service. They don't like the look of the new cleaners you hired to help you, there goes your business with them.

This is not so with commercial clients. They'll sign one-year, two-year contracts with you and cleaning is not a luxury, it's a necessity for their business. Lawyers and doctors don't want to be cleaning toilets at the end of the day!

Residential clients spend less. Commercial cleaning contracts are typically much larger than residential cleans. Invoices of $2000 or $5000 a month per client is not uncommon in commercial cleaning.

Even $20,000 to $50,000 per month for a client is not unusual. The average spend of a residential client is closer to about $200 per month.

The commercial cleaning market is huge. I mean really, really huge. Billions of dollars get spent every year and in every country on cleaning.

But the real magic is in the simple power of the numbers.

Let's say when I'm starting, I'm just looking for extra income. I could drive an Uber. I could get a part-time job. Or I could get a handful of office cleaning contracts. With Uber or a part-time job, I'm trading my time for dollars and own nothing. The business isn't mine. It's my boss' or Uber's. Instead, I could get some office cleaning contracts to clean myself or better still find and train staff, so I don't need to even work at night. Generally speaking, if you know how to win profitable contracts you'll earn much more on an hourly rate than most high-paying jobs.

And an extra $2000–$7000 per month can be a gamechanger for many people.

But it doesn't stop there.

Let's say I just target small offices that have monthly billing of $1000 to keep the math simple. Each office on average might require four hours of cleaning a week. Let's say I use my lunch breaks or take half a day off each week to quote new work and win one extra contract a month. A very achievable target if you are following the right system – we have partners who consistently win over ten to twenty new accounts in a month.

Your business would look like this:

Month 1: $1000

Month 2: $1000 + $1000

Month 3: $1000 + $1000 + $1000

If you do this for an entire year

Month 12: $12,000 per month or $144,000 per year

For 2 years: $24,000 per month or $288,000 per year.

For 3 years: $36,000 per month or $432,000 per year.

This is the power of compounding monthly contract income.

Where I come from in Australia, a university degree or college degree takes on average three years. I don't remember meeting any fresh college graduate making over $400K in their first job!

For many people this is life-changing money. And this can all be done initially on a part-time basis without jeopardizing your day job.

The great part about this is you're only making, in this example one sale a month. In fact, you could stop making sales and you'd still be making money every month.

Unlike many other businesses that constantly require sales every month to stay alive, you're simply plodding along adding one account at a time in this scenario.

PRO TIP

Albert Einstein called compound interest the eighth wonder of the world.

You get to tap into the power of compounding by adding one cleaning contract onto another.

Over time you can end up building a significant size business without any increase in your sales or marketing activity. Very few businesses have this advantage.

Now, obviously when you get to a certain size you are going to need staff. But there's profit here for you to grow that business and have money after paying all your expenses. You're going to be targeting profitable accounts only.

A commercial cleaning business is unlike many other businesses, such as coffee shops and restaurants. In most businesses you have no certainty around sales each month. Every month, in fact, every day you start with zero sales.

You might be able to predict it from last month's sales, but there's no certainty. There's nothing contractually binding a customer in these businesses to come back to your coffee shop or restaurant. You just have to try and encourage repeat customers. Every month starts with zero sales.

Commercial cleaning is different.

Offices prefer to outsource their cleaning and they'll sign cleaning contracts.

These contracts can be as long as one or two years, sometimes even longer. They'll renew these contracts too because once they find a cleaning service that works for them, they don't want to change.

What this means is you can build revenue month on month by simply adding new cleaning contracts onto your existing contracts. Even before the month begins, a commercial cleaning business can predict with relative certainty what their income will be because of the contractual and ongoing nature of the business.

Even with very small contracts the income can build rapidly with the right consistent activity over a number of years.

I've made, however, three big assumptions in this chapter.

The first assumption is that you know how to win a contract. The second is you can keep a contract. And the third assumption is that the contracts are worth winning in the first place – namely that they're profitable.

To turn the numbers into reality, we need a predictable method of acquiring new contracts that are profitable and a system of retention that ensures high customer satisfaction.

In the following chapters, I'm going to cover what fundamentals you must have in place to operate a successful cleaning business.

CHAPTER 5:

Getting the Fundamentals Right

CHAPTER 5:
GETTING THE FUNDAMENTALS RIGHT

"Get the fundamentals down, and the level of everything you do will rise." – Michael Jordan

The analogy I use to describe what's required to run a successful commercial cleaning business is a three-legged stool. A cleaning business is made up of three core pillars or legs that if you get right give you the foundation necessary to build a business. It's a base or seat if you like to pile cleaning contracts on. If you only have one or two of these legs your business won't be stable, predictable or profitable.

These legs are:

Leg 1: A Predictable Quantity of Profitable Cleaning Contracts

Leg 2: A Consistent Delivery of Service

Leg 3: Strong Client Relationships

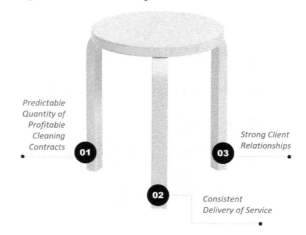

Predictable Quantity of Profitable Cleaning Contracts **01**

Strong Client Relationships **03**

Consistent Delivery of Service **02**

Nearly everything related to running and operating a cleaning business can be boiled down to these legs.

The first leg relates to getting business and business worth having. The other legs relate to keeping business.

There is no point winning business if you can't keep it. And it doesn't matter how well you can look after and retain clients if you don't know how to get them in the first place.

Let's go over each of these legs.

PRO TIP

The three legs of the stool is a deceptively simple concept.

It seems so obvious. But even as you grow a sizable business, the business is always about refining and developing one if not all three of the legs.

Leg 1. A Predictable Quantity of Profitable Cleaning Contracts.

We want profitable cleaning contracts first and foremost.

However, if a client does not have flexibility in their cleaning budget, there will be a ceiling on our profit margins and downward pressure on prices.

Over a certain value, and in most markets, that threshold is around $300,000 a year, greater attention is paid to the cost of cleaning. There will be greater scrutiny over cleaning prices also when a cleaning bill approaches the cost of a full-time salary.

So, an important question to ask before starting your business is what cleaning clients should you be targeting.

Your target market will determine how you develop your service and your value proposition. Most of all it will determine your profit margins.

If you come from the commercial cleaning industry and you've not owned a commercial cleaning business before, you may have been a subcontractor or an employee and dreamt of winning your own large cleaning contract. You might have looked at larger cleaning contracts like shopping malls, airports and thought, "if only I could own one of those contracts, I'd be set for life".

Sorry to be the bearer of bad news, but that is not the case.

They look attractive. They're big. And yes, the revenue can be large. A cleaning contract for a shopping mall could be worth $2 million or more a year.

But in business what matters is the money we take home. The money we put in our pocket after all of our expenses is what counts in the end. Gross revenue can give us bragging rights. Profit pays the bills.

Large contracts like these tend to have low margins. Sometimes very low margins.

We're talking single digits. They can be as low as 2% or 3%. Some of the biggest commercial cleaning companies in the world operate on 1% or 2% profit margins. They service very large government tenders, and large private contracts, such as airports, and major hospitals.

They are playing a volume and low margin game. If you're trading less than $10 million, it's not worth it. You may decide it's not worth it no matter how big you become.

But if your business is only turning over a couple hundred thousand dollars a year or even a million dollars a year, there's no way you can run a viable business operating at 1, 2 or 3% margins.

You've got to have nice, big, fat, healthy margins to make your business viable. If you're turning over a billion dollars, which some of these very large cleaning businesses do, a couple percent in profit is not that bad. You could live with it. It doesn't leave much room for error, but 1% of a billion is still $10 million in profit.

The margins for large contracts are typically low. You have to cover two or three months of wages because you don't get paid straight away. You will need upfront costs for equipment and machinery. So, you can be putting up hundreds of thousands of dollars in these very large contracts before you receive a single dollar of payment from your client and there's often operational complexities around executing and managing large-scale sites.

In short, you're looking at low margins, high upfront costs and a high degree of operational complexity.

The revenue may look attractive. You might have boasting rights. Other cleaning companies could even be envious of you. But these are not the kind of contracts you want to be winning, especially at the start of your business.

What we want instead are highly profitable, easy to execute cleans, what I like to call low-tech high-margin cleaning.

And this is going to be found primarily in small, medium-size offices. This does not necessarily mean we are dealing only with small and medium-size businesses, just that their cleaning requirements aren't large or significant compared to the size of their business.

We are talking about sites that range from $150 a month, which would be a tiny once per fortnight or once per month clean, to sites of up to $20,000 per month for larger premises that require daily cleaning.

Once we go beyond that, contracts become competitive and start to experience margin compression.

The cleaning bill can be one of a shopping mall's largest bills and it attracts a lot of scrutiny and price pressure. It's a significant budget item. Shopping malls will be sensitive to price. And because the bill will be large, tenders for shopping malls are competitive.

This is not the place to start your business.

Instead, we want clients who place importance on cleaning and have the budget flexibility to pay for a premium service.

An example we've mentioned earlier is a lawyer's office.

A lawyer's office could comprise a small two-level office with 25 desks. Now, I don't know many solicitors that earn less than a $100,000 a year.

So it'd be a reasonable expectation that the legal firm would be spending at least $2 million a year in salaries. But this is not a big office. Depending on the scope, fixtures and level of detail required in the clean this could be a five night a week clean, taking an average of two hours a night. Let's say on average it requires 50 hours of cleaning every month.

We could charge anywhere from $2000 to $3000 per month, perhaps even more. This is only $24,000 or $36,000 a year. The amount is insignificant compared to their revenue and expenses.

The reality is cleaning matters to a business such as this. And they stand to lose much more than $24,000 if the cleaning and hygiene is not up to standard. It's not going to have a big impact financially on them if they pay an additional $250 extra a week to get a great service that meets their expectations. The difference, though, between receiving $24,000 and $36,000 for the same job makes a dramatic difference to the profitability of your business.

Clients such as these will pay extra to get the service that exactly meets their needs rather than save a little only to have continuous dramas and problems with their cleaning service.

A legal firm will have security and confidentiality requirements that need to be met. Lack of hygiene will cause staff absence due to sickness that can cost the firm lost billing hours. A dirty office will affect staff morale and affect the perception people have of the business. They certainly would not want high value clients potentially worth hundreds of thousands of dollars a year to them, choosing not to do business with because of a dirty, musty smelling boardroom.

They will happily pay the extra.

These are the clients we want. Clients who value service over price.

The great news is that these clients make up the majority of the commercial cleaning market.

The important thing is to make sure we don't chase clients just for revenue's sake. It's the money left in our pocket after all costs and expenses that counts.

Revenue is vanity. Profit is sanity. Cash flow is reality.

Once we have identified that a client can spend extra money and are willing to do so for the right service, we need to present ourselves as the service they're looking for and demonstrate without a shadow of doubt we can deliver on our promises.

This is exactly what I did when I asked my 'A' grade client what a perfect cleaning service looked like to them and designed my service entirely around what they wanted.

This immediately improved my profit margins and my sales conversions.

My contracts were profitable and my conversion rates predictable. I knew a certain percentage of my cleaning proposals would convert to signed contracts and because I was delivering exactly what they wanted I won them at higher-than-normal rates. My prices were typically 30% higher than competing bids and I'd still win them.

So far, we've solved sales conversions and winning business at profit.

It's no good having a high sales conversion rate if you have few sales opportunities to convert. Even if your sales conversion rate is 100%, if you only have one sales opportunity, you can only ever make one sale.

We need quantity. And a quantity of contracts that are close to each other. In the next chapter, I'm going to show you how to get commercial cleanings and build a pipeline of new business.

CONTRACT

CHAPTER 6:
Getting Cleaning Contracts

CHAPTER 6:
GETTING CLEANING CONTRACTS

"You miss 100% of the shots you don't take." – *Wayne Gretzky*

Let's talk about leads and filling up a sales pipeline of new cleaning contracts.

Search engine optimization works. Search engine marketing works. Lead platforms work. Telemarketing works. Even LinkedIn messaging can be used to generate leads.

All these methods cost money, take time and have limits. Only so many people, for instance in a given area, will search out cleaning services. It won't matter how much you spend on Google ads there will always be a limit to the number of leads.

However the biggest problem with the methods of lead generation just mentioned is that you'll have leads spread out over a large geographic area. This makes planning profitable and efficient job runs difficult. You'll be tempted to focus only on larger cleans because of this, making you lose out on the very profitable small cleans. This is what led me to wanting to sell parts of my business.

The answer would seem to be door-to-door appointment setting, either in person or on the phone.

I tried this when I started and failed miserably. I knocked on businesses, introduced myself and my company and asked if they were happy with their current cleaners and interested in a proposal. I would need to knock on nearly 40 doors to get one person half interested in accepting a proposal from me. They were long demoralizing days. Rejection after rejection took its toll and I didn't continue this method for long even after trying lots of gimmicks offering free cleans and trials.

Calling businesses to set appointments was not much better. I would need to call about 60 businesses using a similar script to get a sales appointment.

However, I viewed telemarketing as a way to scale lead generation. And it did do that to a degree. I built a small team of telemarketers who could set one to two appointments per day for each of our sales team. It was expensive. It was hard to manage. Telemarketers, especially the good ones, can be prima donnas. If you're in the same office as them, you'll have to deal with their emotional rollercoaster rides as they deal with rejection after rejection then finally get an appointment. No word of a lie, I had one that would tell everyone to hide the knives if they didn't have an appointment by the afternoon.

But we got appointments with telemarketing and won business.

We ran lots of experiments and tested new approaches and scripts. I even hired telemarketing consultants to improve our training and scripts.

One experiment led to a major breakthrough.

We wanted to see if a two step approach would work better than going straight for an appointment in the first conversation with a decision maker.

The tactic was to survey them first to see how satisfied they were with their current cleaners. We asked them if they were open to other options and cleaning service providers, while making it clear we would not be asking them for an appointment on that call. The intention was to send those that were open to options some information that would lead them to asking for an appointment for us to quote their cleaning.

The experiment didn't work as planned. We saw no significant uptake in sales appointments compared to the more direct method.

But what we learnt running this experiment surprised all of us.

Over 70% of people said that they weren't 100% satisfied with the service they were getting and that they were open to alternatives.

This confused us at first because nowhere near 7 out of 10 people wanted to set a sales appointment. On a good day we would get 1 in 30 people to say yes to an appointment. Our strike rate on appointments from calls was closer to 3% not 70%.

I thought maybe we just called the wrong area. We tried in other areas and other cities. Still, over 70% of people were dissatisfied and open to change.

It didn't add up.

If there was so much dissatisfaction, why was it so hard to get a sales appointment?

I only had to recall the many conversations I had had with prospective clients to understand one major reason.

They were suspicious and skeptical. They had been promised the world before, only to be let down. Many had gone through a number of cleaners over the years, only to be disappointed. The service would typically start out great then slowly deteriorate and become as bad or worse than the cleaners they fired.

They had become resigned to the substandard service that was common due to the low barrier to entry to the cleaning industry. Anyone with a cloth and mop could call themselves a cleaner and start a cleaning company.

A lot of clients had accepted this mediocrity. They didn't want to go through the hassle of changing cleaners only to be disappointed again or risk changing to worse cleaners. It seemed safer to stay with the devil they knew. At least they knew their current cleaners weren't leaving doors unlocked or burning the place down.

Despite this fact, businesses still did accept sales appointments and changed cleaners. So, it could not explain entirely why appointments were so difficult to get.

I realized the approach I was taking – and the approach that was standard in the cleaning industry –was wrong.

I was making it hard to say yes to a proposal, making it all about me and not them, and making too big a deal about getting a set appointment to send a proposal.

In short, my approach was far too salesy and asked far too much too soon from a prospective customer.

This is how a typical interaction went if we canvassed at the door or called for an appointment.

> "Hi, my name is Damien from Urban Clean. We're calling in on you because we clean a number of clients around here and I was wondering if you're happy with your current cleaner and would like a proposal from us?"

> "No, sorry we're busy right now and happy with our current cleaners."

> "I'm happy to give you a quote, it would take no more than 5–10 mins"

> "No sorry we're not interested and actually really busy at the moment. We're under contract anyway."

Some 90% of the conversations would go this way – nowhere.

Everything about this approach and script was wrong. Strangers don't care about your name, your company, who else you service or what you want. If you come in like this, you're an uninvited and unwelcome interruption to their day.

The whole interaction was about us, what we wanted from them, and our needs only.

There is nothing social about it. In fact, it's positively antisocial. And people wonder why cold calling doesn't work when they use scripts and approaches like this.

What we need is a social approach. We want to make a quick connection and be seen as a welcome distraction not an uninvited interruption.

Introducing the Method I Used to Get 20 Contracts in 30 Days

Compare the last conversation with an interaction like this.

> "I was just next door doing a cleaning assessment for Tony at Acme Consulting and thought it would be silly for me not to drop in and see how we could help you with your cleaning too."
>
> "Oh, we've actually already got cleaners."
>
> "Okay that's great. Things can change though."
>
> "That's true."
>
> "Why don't I flick across some details, so you've got them nice and easy at your fingertips?"
>
> "Sure, you can send us some information."
>
> "What's the best email to send that to?"

At this point a few additional carefully scripted questions will lead them to sharing details on the frequency of the cleaning, their specific needs and scope of work. Very often you'll get an opportunity to walk through their premises and have all the information you need to send an accurate cleaning proposal.

I call this the Quick Connect Method.

Door to door marketing in this way is predictable, scalable and fast. It's the cornerstone, the bread and butter if you like of a successful janitorial marketing campaign.

So why does it work?

PRO TIP

Talk to most marketing agencies and they'll tell you that cold calling is dead.

Dumb cold calling was always dead.

Smart cold calling has grown global businesses.

The "cold calling is dead" myth has been bought by nearly every lazy salesperson. Don't drink this kool-aid.

Direct marketing is not always financially viable because you don't know if you're communicating with your target audience. You waste a lot of time marketing, talking and advertising to people who will never need or want what you sell. Not so with commercial cleaning. You can identify your target audience from the street. Open up Google Maps and look for the gray roofs. That's where the office parks and industrial precincts are and where you'll find your future customers. Not every product or service has this advantage.

You can send them direct mail, phone them or visit them. Most direct mail will get thrown in the bin. Phone calls have the advantage of speed. You can dial a lot of numbers in a short space of time. You only need a small number of people to say yes to an appointment so long as you're making enough calls. And those people are more likely open to changing services. Or you can visit them virtually on the phone and get them to give you enough details to send them a proposal.

A visit has the advantage of the 'in front of them' effect. It's easy to throw mail in the bin. You can fob someone off on the phone. It's hard to do that in person. You don't need to be as skillful a writer or talker in person so long as your approach is friendly, social and strategic. In this case you'll be a distraction office managers want, not an unwelcome interruption to their day.

The last approach works. It's social. It's not awkward or uncomfortable and there's no manipulation involved.

You don't introduce yourself by your name, your company or what you want from them. It's direct. It makes sense why you're there and you've got 'neighbor equity'. Someone right next door to you thought it was okay to speak with you, therefore it's safe for them to do the same.

You're there to help and you're not there to tell them why their current cleaners are so bad and why they should use you. Instead, you let your professional approach and the dissatisfaction in the market do the heavy lifting for you.

So, you've collected information. You've uncovered needs. You know the cleaning scope, the elements and size of the clean. Now you need to demonstrate you are the solution that your prospective clients have been looking for.

An invaluable tool is a cleaning calculator that relates cleaning production rates to hours cleaned. This will give you a monthly fixed price based on the hourly rates and profit margin you're targeting.

It's essential that a price is put into a proposal and that proposal is sent out, preferably within minutes or the same day as your visit. We built a cleaning calculator and proposal creator that can accurately calculate prices and write professional bespoke proposals within minutes and for simple accounts within seconds even.

Your proposal should address your experience, capability, the scope, cleaning schedule, service agreement and price.

In the body of your proposal, you must show you understand what matters to them and demonstrate how:

- Specific items important to that client are addressed.

- Consistent standards are maintained.

- Communication happens between cleaners, staff and management.

- All stakeholders can see that jobs are carried out according to scope by authorized, trained and compliant staff with appropriate insurances, licenses and checks.

- All property, staff and confidential information are kept safe, confidential and secure.

- Your cleaning service can provide value above and beyond simple cleaning.

The key is to demonstrate, not tell. Don't say you provide real time reporting. Show samples of real time notifications and reports. Give them access to a reporting dashboard.

Provide testimonials and case studies. There should be undeniable proof your service is exactly what you say it is. Remember it's not that they are happy with the service already being provided to them – 70% of them we know aren't. They are just skeptical that you're any different to the service they already have.

Your proposal will do some work of convincing them that you are different. And a great proposal will get some conversions. It won't be enough by itself to get strong sales conversion rates.

With the right proposal they'll be able to see you're professional and have serviced clients well in the past. But your past clients and case studies aren't them. They want proof you'll be right for them and their business!

Promising to send proposals and doing so promptly will help build trust. Doing just that is going to put you in front of 90% of other clients. But to close business, you need to do more.

Take notes of everything you see that could be improved with their cleaning. Listen to problems and challenges that they are facing keeping their premises clean.

Write a list of tools, resources and solutions that could help them. Then go do it for them, even before they choose to spend money with you.

I have sent boxes of hand sanitizers because an office manager was worried, they didn't have enough for all their staff. I have cleaned windows, provided a catalog of industrial mats, tested chemicals to see if they would remove stains.

Some of our partners take this to extreme levels. One of our partners wanted to close a cleaning contract for a chain of 24-hour gyms that they happened to be a member of. Their current cleaners couldn't remove a build-up of black grime in the gym bathroom floors. This partner let themselves in at night, filmed themselves cleaning the tiles, showed on camera the dirty black water that came off the tiles. They forwarded this video to the gym manager in the morning. They won the cleaning contract for the entire group.

This kind of follow-up is radical, separates you from all other competition and closes sales.

Our cleaning contract acquisition was now predictable and profitable and business was won in volume.

A member of our sales team could approach 20 businesses in the same street, send 15 proposals, and be confident of winning at least one contract. This could be done in a single day too. There was still a sales cycle and the laws of averages, but this new method meant we could build a pipeline of proposals, and be confident of winning business day in and day out every month.

Are there other ways of generating leads and proposals? Yes, there are. In fact, while approaching new businesses you will be building a significant size database of potential new clients. If you communicate with them regularly providing them valuable content, people will reach out to you at a later date when they're ready to change cleaners.

As your business matures too, you'll build strategic partnerships with other trades and professionals. You'll get access to their clients and prospects. You'll start to get referrals. You may even be selected to place a tender bid because of the reputation you've built for superior service and delivery.

These methods of lead generation together with the Quick Connect Method will build you a pipeline of proposals and prospects. Once you've mastered this you'll never be short on new business or hoping for business to somehow fall into your lap.

CHAPTER 7:

Other Methods of Marketing

CHAPTER 7:
OTHER METHODS OF MARKETING

"The most dangerous number in business is the number one." – Dan Kennedy

You can tell from my last chapter that I'm a huge advocate of direct marketing using the Quick Connect Method. There is no better way to grow your business.

That doesn't mean there is no value in building and developing other marketing channels. As the famous marketer Dan Kennedy wrote, the most dangerous number in business is the number one. One supplier, one distributor, one marketing strategy leads businesses one step away from one bad stroke of luck. It would be remiss of me not to cover the other methods of acquiring new cleaning contracts.

Telemarketing

This is a method of marketing that works but one I don't recommend. By telemarketing, what I mean is someone calls a number of businesses to get someone to agree to a set appointment where you get a chance to do a walkthrough and pitch before you send them a proposal.

There are a number of reasons I don't recommend this. With telemarketing your cost of acquisition nearly doubles as it requires two people to make a sale. You need someone on the phone ringing people up during the day to set appointments, and somebody who's going to go to those set appointments.

Telemarketing makes salespeople lazy. They don't feel responsible for prospecting. A good telemarketer can set on average two appointments a day. Some days they might set three, other days only one. Sometimes none.

It's not unusual even for a good telemarketer to go through a dry patch and set only one or two appointments for the week. Salespeople are the masters of excuses. If you don't have any appointments for them, it's likely they're not going to do anything and they're going to say to themselves, "I didn't get any appointments, I'll go home early today." And let's be honest, if you're that salesperson, and the telemarketers don't set any leads for you, and you're used to getting set appointments, is it likely you're going to go out and generate your own activity? Not likely.

If you insist on having telemarketers, don't outsource. Your definition of a quality appointment will be different from an outsourced company. Before developing the Quick Connect Method, we outsourced and directly employed telemarketers. It only worked when we employed our own team of appointment setters. I especially don't advise outsourcing to overseas operations based in countries like the Philippines or in India. People pick it up straight away that they're not talking to a local business, and they don't like it. I had one outsourced provider have their telemarketers pretend to confirm 'already set' appointments. I suspected something was off with the set appointments, but when one of them called our own office to confirm a set appointment for a cleaning walkthrough that we had never set, we knew exactly why people were confused when we turned up for a quote!

There are many business functions that can be outsourced to cheaper overseas suppliers where salaries are significantly lower than in developed countries like the United States, Canada and Australia. Telemarketing is not one of them. A telemarketer will struggle to set appointments for you if they follow a script in a robotic fashion or have a strong heavy accent. A good telemarketer will use empathy. They'll have a nuanced approach to every conversation. Tonality in these conversations matters. It's not likely you're going to find any of that from a non-native speaker that's outsourced overseas.

You need callers who can show empathy on the phone. It's a skill. It's not easy to do day in and day out. The good ones will be demanding employees. Outbound appointment setting is a tough gig. Some days appointment setters are on top of the world. The conversations flow easy, and appointments come thick and fast. Other days, not so. No one wants to talk to them. No one's interested in a walkthrough. The appointment-setters feel demoralized and fall into a pit of despair. They're not easy employees to manage either. The levelheaded ones, for some reason, don't get as many leads. Maybe it's something about the constant rejection that grinds people down and it takes a certain type of personality to do it well. Don't say I didn't warn you.

The last reason I don't recommend telemarketing is that you're going to send proposals to people who would have said yes to a set appointment anyway using the Quick Connect Method. But you are going to miss out on everyone who isn't quite ready to change cleaners but maybe would if they had the right proposal in front of them. That's about 95% of everyone you call. The Quick Connect Method allows you to send proposals to people who weren't ever going to agree to a set appointment all while building a qualified database.

SEO

This is a long game and highly competitive. Beware of the false promises that marketing agencies make. It will take time, effort and a boatload of money. First and second spots or SERPS as they're called are hard to get with no guarantees of success.

PRO TIP

Once you find your primary means of lead generation, find other ways to supplement and diversify your marketing.

This just makes good business sense.

Don't get me wrong: a one or two spot listing is great to get, it's just not the holy grail of marketing some marketing agencies want you to believe it is. Even if you were able to achieve a first page listing in Google, it won't necessarily make your business take off or achieve a greater result than direct marketing. A worst-case scenario is you spend hundreds of thousands of dollars and countless hours to move your website listing from 100th place to second page. In this case you've wasted your money completely. As the saying goes, where's a good place to bury a dead body? On the second page of Google. A great result is to have your website rank one or two for a few high-traffic keywords. This will give you a regular source of leads.

Start by researching keywords relevant to your business with high traffic. You'll need to create great content and localized pages. There are technical aspects you'll need to get right such as headlines, tags, on page optimization and metatags. Be prepared for it to take at least six months or longer to rank for any high-traffic keyword.

Another strategy is to target long tail keywords. These could be searches such as 'how to remove gum from office car parks' or 'best carpet cleaning businesses in Henderson, Las Vegas'. These searches won't get as many searches as 'janitorial business Las Vegas' but there is much less competition for these keywords which makes it easier to get the top one or two listings. Low search volumes though mean you'd have to target many of these searches to get any volume of leads.

Oh, and don't try to cheat your way to high ranking – otherwise known as black hat SEO. The algorithms are smart. Even if you beat them for a little while, they'll get you in the end.

Be aware that search engine algorithms constantly change and strategies that may have worked in the past, won't work now. The advancement of chat AIs such as OpenAI's ChatGPT could also make search engine rankings go the way of Yellow Pages in the future.

SEM

Google Ads and Bing allow you to buy sponsored listings. They let you pay to advertise on keyword searches and get at the top of search engine results.

Google Ads isn't cheap. This is why having an organic listing is so valuable. It is also difficult to get a large volume of leads with this method. Paid search listings get a significantly smaller number of click throughs than the top one or two organic listings. There's less trust with sponsored listings than organic rankings. There is also always going to be a limit on the eyeballs you catch even if you have an unlimited budget. Even with a budget of $10,000 or $20,000, it's not likely you will get a chance to spend it in a population area of 1 to 2 million people. And that's going to be the case even if you have a highly optimized campaign with great negative keywords. With an optimized campaign you're still going to have to weed out some unwanted inquiries and people clicking on your website that aren't your buyers. They could be your competitors, but also residential inquiries, one off cleaning requests and job inquiries.

Paid search can be used to supplement your marketing efforts and build credibility with a prospective client since they see your business on multiple platforms.

LinkedIn

Most Social Media platforms are not going to be effective to use for winning commercial cleaning contracts. The exception to this is LinkedIn. Nearly all your prospects will be on LinkedIn. It is currently and for the foreseeable future the largest social media platform for professionals. The simplest strategy is to connect to as many office managers in your area and let them know you're available to help them with anything related to their cleaning. You will get engagement, but you will need to make many connections and send many messages to get someone to ask for a cleaning quote. This is time consuming and LinkedIn even with their paid sales navigator subscription puts limits on the number of connections and interactions you're allowed to have.

An alternative to this direct approach is to use it to supplement your other marketing activities and create awareness and authority with your prospects.

After collecting business cards, connect with them on LinkedIn. Again, another platform and touchpoint to build credibility and awareness of you and your business. Be sure to post success stories about clients and your team, most importantly give valuable content that helps solve their current problems and shows you solving them for your clients.

This will keep you top of mind and build your expert status and authority with your prospective clients.

Email Database

If you're using the Quick Connect Method to send out proposals and build a pipeline of business, you'll find most people are not yet ready to change cleaners. They may have just recently changed, they may be currently very happy or under contract. But they have given us permission to send information and a proposal. So even after you've followed up without immediate success, they can become part of your email database.

And things change.

Their current cleaner could drop the ball, they could be nearing the end of their contract, they could be reviewing their contract agreements and contracts. If you send them regular emails with valuable content, you'll be front of mind when they go look for another cleaner. Tips about hygiene, cleaning, quick guides and success stories have worked well for us. Get video testimonials from businesses that are your clients and email them to neighboring businesses. Segment your list into different industries and send content that's valuable specifically to gyms, medical centers, schools or professional offices.

Over time this database will become a valuable asset to your business and a continuous source of leads.

Referral Program

What's the secret to referrals? Ask, ask, ask. Of course, you must be referable. Your service can't just be excellent, it needs to be remarkable. Do the unexpected – provide birthday cards, create a loyalty club, go over and above in the delivery of your service. Create surprises and delights such as free mints and chocolate on desks, in meeting rooms and reception areas.

With a formal referral program be sure to reward the referee and the referrer. If possible it should look like the referrer is the one providing a gift to the referee. The reward doesn't need to be a cash reward or discount. For instance you might offer both the referee and referrer one or two weeks of cleaning at no cost or provide an additional cleaning service such as a window clean or fridge clean out that's not normally part of your regular cleaning schedule.

Strategic Partnerships

Strategic Partnerships is one of my favorite ways of accelerating business growth. It's especially valuable once you've grown your business or can demonstrate to strategic partners that you can and intend to grow fast. Strategic Partnerships allow you to leverage other businesses' sales and marketing activity, their client list, database, trust and reputation.

If done right, Strategic Partnerships can put a rocket under your business.

Strategic Partners can work for you in two ways. They can introduce you to new clients. And you can make additional sales to your clients using their products and services.

So, what kinds of businesses do you want to partner with?

I divide Strategic Partners into Aggregators and Partner Businesses.

Aggregators include commercial property managers, cost consultants and supply aggregators.

These are companies that source services and suppliers as a procurement and management service.

Partner Businesses are in industry verticals closely related to cleaning.

These are businesses that serve similar clients to you and swim in adjacent lanes.

For instance, building-maintenance-related services and consumable products are closely related to cleaning.

These businesses provide products or services that are natural extensions of cleaning like toilet paper, paper towels, and air fresheners. And you can stretch this to businesses that provide mats, coffee and stationery.

Additional services can include carpet cleaning, strip and sealing, window cleaning and extend to garden care, security and drycleaning.

There are some products and services in lanes too far for a cleaning business.

We're talking about professional services like accounting, bookkeeping, solicitors, marketing, sales and executive coaching.

If you jump too many lanes away from cleaning, you start to lose trust and credibility with a client.

So don't throw around business coaching or accounting or marketing or HR services in front of your clients. Believe me your business could be ten times bigger than theirs but they'll think they know more than you on these topics and have better connections than you because hey, you're just a cleaning company in their mind.

So you want to stick with services and products that are a more natural fit.

A list of potential Partner Businesses could include:

- Painters
- Gardeners
- Security services
- Electricians
- Plumbers
- Lighting professionals
- Waste management providers
- Coffee suppliers
- Stationery suppliers
- Dry cleaners
- Pest controllers
- Shopfitters
- Indoor plant suppliers

This is by no means an exhaustive list. It's just meant to get you thinking.

How do you find these partners?

You can approach them directly. LinkedIn is a perfect tool for this. Be friendly and direct. Don't beat around the bush. Your approach will be different though depending on whether they are an aggregator or partner business.

Remember this is a relationship not a one-time transaction so you'll need to approach it that way.

For a Partner Business I might reach out with a message like

- I have customers looking for your service. I'm looking to partner with a business that provides ....x..., shall we jump on a quick call and see if we can help each other?

Alternatively, you can Google businesses and make phone calls. These aren't hard phone calls either – people will want to chat if there's the prospect of additional business or money coming their way.

With Supply Aggregators such as commercial real estate agents, it's likely they have a lot of suppliers vying for their attention so your approach needs to be a little different.

The main thing is to stand out from everyone else. Make more of an effort than your competition. You could send them a gold envelope. Send lumpy mail – put in gimmicky gifts with engaging messages.

Your aim is to get them to call you back and arrange a coffee meeting.

My favorite method of all to find partners is networking.

Go to Chamber of Commerce meetings, business meetups, join BNI, any local business networking events for that matter.

Now here's the thing – and it's a massive mistake people new to networking make – don't go to these events to find clients. Go to find partners.

And give first. Connect people with others that can help them. Have an attitude of service, seek to understand other businesses needs first before suggesting you know how you can help them.

Also, the people you really want to meet may not be at the event in the room. But almost always someone in that room can introduce you to someone outside the room that you need to meet. This is how I've met some of our best strategic partners.

Don't rush either, spend time with them. Become their friends. Catch up for lunch and dinner. Invite them to social events. You want to know if you can get along. If you can trust them and what their values are. I like to do a small deal with people first and if that goes well, begin collaborating in a bigger way.

You can even create your own networking events and business meetups with your existing clients and get them to invite other business owners to it. Organize a speaker, make it a wine and cheese night – heck even get sponsors to pay for it.

Okay, so you've found some people you can work with.

How do we work with them?

First let's talk about Partner Businesses then we'll discuss Aggregators. Each month you'll be providing an audit to your customers. In a later chapter we'll talk about why these are so important to keeping your existing business, but they also serve as a great sales tool.

Your monthly audit reports are like mini proposals you give to your clients every month. And it's your chance to upsell.

Once you've audited the cleaning, and audited compliance, there should be a section that provides suggestions and site recommendations.

This is where you can list the products and services of your strategic partners. I like to provide pricing. This means you're providing a real quote they can approve and add onto their next month's bill.

You could, if you wanted, have a rebate arrangement with the suppliers. This is where they invoice the client directly and pay you a commission. But most times it's easier to add a markup and add it to your cleaning invoice. Clients prefer it this way and you'll retain more control as well. It's also likely you'll get a greater percentage working this way. You can markup services anywhere from 15–40% and sometimes more. Most supply partners won't give more than 10% as a rebate and you're now reliant on them doing the right thing each month. And even if they're honest, it's an admin burden that they may not be set up for.

Now if I've agreed to partner with these businesses, I want to make sure I'm referring them and connecting them to potential new business.

I don't try to get a clip out of these sales. I see this as part of building goodwill and cementing the relationship.

Now let's talk Aggregators – I'm talking about cost consultants, property managers and service aggregators.

With these businesses, I want to leverage commercial cleaning's biggest advantage – regular contractual income.

I consider them an extension of my sales team and I want them incentivized. So, I offer a monthly contract percentage rebate. Sometimes this is not necessary because their business model is to invoice clients with a markup – but even if this is happening I like to give a small rebate to them which they can keep themselves or even pass on to their clients.

Small percentage splits work well for businesses that don't normally receive anything ongoing. For instance builders of office fit outs. They love getting recurring revenue like this.

Cost consultants are great too. A lot of cost consultants make money by charging a percentage that the client saves typically over a two-year period. If you can offer the cost consultant a trailing percentage that lasts for the life of the contract, you can be sure they'll be interested in putting your business in front of their clients.

There are other strategies too, such as piggyback invoicing where you advertise on their invoices and proposals and vice versa.

So, we covered how to work with partners, what are the mistakes you should avoid:

Mistake #1: Not documenting the arrangement.

Always have agreements signed by you and the strategic partner. This formalizes the partnership and avoids any potential confusion and misunderstandings down the road. It protects both parties.

Mistake #2: Rushing.

It takes time to find the right partners and build trust. You want to be sure they're 100% honest with their dealings. Talk to others that have worked with them in the past. Spend time with them. Take them out for lunch, dinner or a social gathering. Breaking bread is a great way to get to know people and see if there's alignment. You won't be able to build this kind of relationship and rapport in an office environment.

Mistake #3: Wrong fit.

As much as it might be exciting to align yourself with a national building maintenance group, can you service all their business on a national level? The answer could be yes if you're national or part of a national group. But if not, it could be difficult. In other instances, you could be too big for them. You've got to make sure they can service your clients, and you can service theirs. You have to deliver well, and you have to be in a position to take on the opportunities they bring your way.

And lastly, always do the right thing. Don't try to work around your agreement. Be the person you'd want to partner with. If you get the work because of them, pay them. It will be noticed. You'll get more opportunities and more partners.

Don't try and drive hard bargains. It's got to be a win–win–win arrangement. It's got to work for you, for them, and the client.

Strategic partnerships can rapidly accelerate the growth of your business. Every cleaning business that's serious about making more money and expanding their business should be actively looking for and working with strategic partners.

You must be intentional about strategic partnerships. Great ones don't just happen. You need to be persistent, patient and work a plan.

CHAPTER 8:

Even More Ways to Market Your Cleaning Business

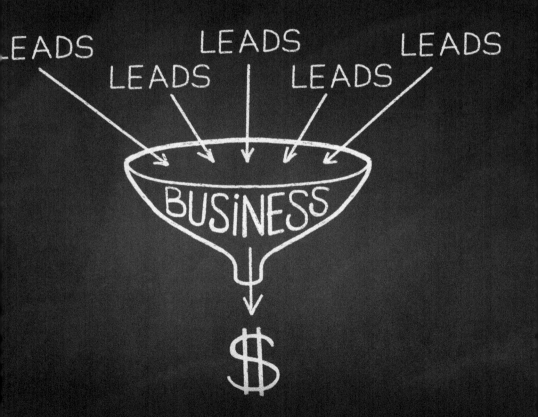

CHAPTER 8:
EVEN MORE WAYS TO MARKET YOUR CLEANING BUSINESS

"I find the harder I work, the luckier I am." – Thomas Jefferson

And there are still more ways to market your cleaning business!

Tenders

Most government work will be won through public tenders. Large private companies often invite selected cleaning companies to take part in a request for tender (RFT). And sometimes these tenders are public and open to everyone.

Without a prior relationship or existing track record with the tender procurer, it's a numbers game. Often it will take many attempts to win your first government tender as you are yet to show a track record as a supplier with the government. You need to win at least one to break the ice.

Tenders can be extremely competitive and in most cases, tenders are price sensitive with the lowest bidders winning. I once attended a walkthrough for a government tender where there were over 45 other cleaning companies present.

Here's a few tips to help you win cleaning tenders:

- Have great client references that also give evidence of your experience servicing jobs similar to the tender you're bidding on.

- Have an extensive list of jobs demonstrating your experience and expertise.

- Make sure your tender document is easy to read, well organized and free from error. Remember the readers and assessors are likely to be detail oriented and will judge spelling, grammar and formatting mistakes harshly.

- Your pricing must be spot on. You must know how other companies price and calculate production rates. To be in the running you'll need to be within a 5% range of the majority of established and experienced bidders. You are more likely to win if you're in the lower section of these prices. If your price is very low, they'll want an explanation otherwise they'll suspect that you're not meeting the cleaning scope or paying staff and contractors legally.

- Make sure you read, understand and answer all the questions they require from you, and that you provide all the information in the way they ask for it to be presented or formatted.

Tenders are not for the faint of heart. Cleaning businesses that derive most of their work from tenders will have a team of tender writers and cost estimators. Profit margins are low and due to the size of the contracts they can be difficult and complex to execute well.

Top 100 list

This is my preferred method of winning larger clients. You select your ideal 100 clients and work through a set attraction and follow-up sequence designed to gain their attention and trust, in order to get an opportunity to do business with them.

These are the kinds of clients that just having ten of them would radically change the reputation and size of your cleaning business.

Creative marketing is the key here. For instance, you could send a parcel with a fake arm in it with an attached note saying you'll give your right arm to have a meeting with them. Or send a drone without the remote. Promise to bring the remote when you meet in person. In all your interactions add value and solve problems.

One of our partners became a preferred supplier for a large property management group just by solving a problem they had with one of the towers they had just taken over managing. They didn't know what the cleaners schedule was or what their scope of works were, and they couldn't get this information out of the cleaning company currently cleaning them. Our partner went to this tower, visited every tenant, found out when the cleaners came and what they did and compiled a spreadsheet with all this information. In addition he created a recommended scope of works and schedule that included periodicals such as carpet cleaning. This saved the property management group days of work and hassle. He only found this information out though by first gaining their attention and then discovering their needs and challenges.

I love this way of winning large clients because not only will you be selected for an RFT should they decide to tender, you have already built a relationship and established your value so price is not going to be the sole deciding factor in your bid.

The important thing to remember about having a top 100 is that this strategy needs time, typically two to three years. It will take longer to get in front of decision makers and you'll need to wait in most cases for their cleaning contracts to come up for renewal.

If you'd like to learn more about creating and marketing to a targeted hit list, I recommend you read the *Ultimate Sales Machine* by the late Chet Holmes, and Dan Kennedy's books especially *Magnetic Marketing* and the *No B.S. Marketing to the Affluent.*

Lead Generation Platforms

Lastly, let's cover lead generation platforms. Service Seeking, Bark, and Oneflare are just a handful that we have in Australia. And there's a good chance that by the time you read this there will be others. Some of these platforms are international and others are country specific. But you will find them in almost any country.

Lead platforms all work on a similar premise. Namely, they're designed to help customers save time searching for services. So, they're going to help match customers with service providers. Service providers typically will buy credits, and they use those credits to access contact details of potential clients who post jobs that they want quotes for. You've got to be quick because normally only three or five businesses are allowed to quote on a single job.

You have to remember that you're going to be competing against three or five other quotes and likely the people who have requested a quote have never landed on your website. They know nothing about you until you come to visit them.

Like SEM, you can win work using these platforms, but expect it to be expensive, competitive and not something that's going to create explosive growth for your business.

A Simple Formula

If you've got this far you may be confused with all the options available to you to win commercial cleaning contracts. Which one should you use? Or which one should I start with?

You need some formulas to make informed decisions.

The Sales Formula in commercial cleaning is simple:

Number of Proposals per Month

X

Conversion Rate of Proposals

X

Average Dollar Sale

X

Conversion Rate

=

Monthly Cleaning Contract Sales

What this formula doesn't take into account is the process and the cost associated with each way of getting a proposal. How you get the opportunity to send a proposal will affect your conversion rate, average dollar sale and rate of growth. The cost of sourcing and producing that proposal is going to be constrained by your budget, cash flow requirements and the profitability you aim at achieving per contract.

To work this out you'll need a Marketing Formula:

Number of Interactions (online requests, conversations, or calls etc.)

X

Conversion Rate to Proposal

=

Number of Proposals

&

Cost per Interaction

/

Conversion Rate to Proposal

=

Cost per Proposal

A proposal generated from a referral is going to have a much higher conversion rate than a proposal generated from a cold call. Its dollar value will be related to the size of the referring business, as businesses tend to refer you to businesses like themselves. The cost of generating that lead is going to be cheaper than a lead generated from paid advertising.

PRO TIP

Marketing isn't a cost. It's an investment.

Marketing is all about generating a return on your investment. Like every investment you've got to examine the numbers.

Some investments are duds, others are no-brainers. It's your job to work out which is which when marketing.

However if you only receive one referral a month, you won't be able to win more than one cleaning contract a month from this source.

What this means is that you'll need to use the formulas above for each method of generating proposals.

Doing this is essential if you have a budget and want to achieve business growth targets.

All marketing methods will have a daily interaction limit regardless of budget. For instance, if you target a geographic area of one million people, on average the number of businesses is 10% of the population, and of that 10% half of those businesses won't be suitable for you to target because they are too small to need a cleaning service. That leaves 50,000 businesses. We severely limit our lead generation volume if we only use inbound marketing channels such as Google Ads. Even though we know that 70% of the market is quietly dissatisfied with the current service they're receiving, if we assume only 3% of the market is actively searching for a cleaning service in any given month that makes only 1500 prospects looking for quotes.

Not all those 1500 will go online or search through Google. And of the ones who do, not all will click on your ad, or request a quote once they land on your website. It's been my experience that a cleaning business will struggle to generate more than 25 qualified online requests per month using Google Ads within a population of a million people. The cost can range from $50 to $250 per proposal. Worse, these leads are going to spread right across the city. Not to mention we're missing out on engaging with 97% of the rest of the market.

And this is where the Quick Connect Method shines. One person can comfortably generate 20 proposals in a day. Even if only 70% of the business you interact with will accept a proposal, the number of proposals that can be sent out in a month is limited in practice only by the number of people out generating and proposals for you. If you do it yourself, it will only cost you your time. If you employ others to do it for you, your growth can be quickly accelerated.

What's great about the Quick Connect Method is that it allows you to build a database that you can later nurture through LinkedIn and email.

CHAPTER 9:

Keeping Business

CHAPTER 9:
KEEPING BUSINESS

"Everything is based on a simple rule: Quality is the best business plan. Period." – Steve Jobs

In the last couple of chapters, we covered the first of the three legs of a successful janitorial business, a predictable quantity of profitable cleaning contracts.

Cold calling is far from dead. Most people don't know how to do it right. Cold calling done right, works. If done right, it gives you a predictable quantity of business coming through. We've got people who are able to win a couple of contracts a week with cold calling. In fact, we've even had people win a couple of contracts a day using the system outlined in the last chapters.

The first leg is about getting business. The last two legs are about retaining cleaning contracts. This chapter is about keeping the business you win.

Those last two legs again are:

- **Consistent Delivery of Service**
- **Strong Client Relationships**

There's no point winning business only to lose it after a few months.

Wealth is made by winning and keeping contracts.

My golfing friends tell me that the game of golf is won or lost with the short game. It's fun to hit the ball 300 yards. A monster drive is impressive. But you're not scored on how far you can hit the ball, scoring in golf is about getting the ball in the hole with as few shots as possible. When pro golfer, Paula Creamer, was asked what made her so successful in golf, she said, "Practice, work out, proper nutrition, and lots of work on my short game. In golf that's really where the strokes come off the scorecard."

When you run a cleaning business it's impressive to win a lot of cleaning contracts. But the game is won or lost on customer retention. Your scorecard is not based on how many contracts you win, but the number of clients you win and keep.

Businesses that provide an exceptional customer experience, that keep their customers just as happy after two years as they do in the first month, are the businesses that win.

The first leg is really about making promises that potential clients want you to make. They have needs, you have solutions to those needs. Based on those promises they are willing to pay more, and choose you instead of other cheaper cleaning companies. People see what you're offering, they see that, "This is the kind of cleaning service we've been looking for, for years. You seem to have the goods." You're making powerful promises, and that's what's getting you the business.

If we hope to keep that business, we must deliver on those promises. And this is what's meant by Consistent Delivery of Service. We must consistently deliver on the promises made to get their business in the first place.

PRO TIP

Retaining business is about delivering on promises.

Keeping customers forever and growing accounts through additional sales and referrals is about doing more than what's expected.

A large part of your promises will be focused on cleaning standards, but there's other things that matter just as much as the cleaning. If you promise a method of communication, you've got to deliver on that method of communication consistently. If you promise auditing, you promise to be transparent, you promise reporting, you promise to be proactive in finding solutions to facilitate needs, you've got to deliver on these things consistently.

Systems are the answer.

You'll need checklists, manuals, auditing systems and training programs. You'll need to lay out every part of the business step by step. All processes should be set out and documented. Nothing can be left to chance. I even built an app that delivered real-time reporting and notifications with image captures of completed tasks.

I'm not going to lie; this takes time and can cost serious money. I went to the extent of creating an integrated management system certified to international ISO 9001 standards for quality control. It's a huge advantage joining a well-developed franchise system that's already invested time and money into creating these systems.

The systems for consistent delivery and constant improvement must relate to the promises made in your marketing and sales. They are not separate.

You make promises, then have systems developed to deliver on those promises.

The last leg is Strong Client Relationships.

Clients are looking for more than just cleaners when they hire a cleaning service. They expect proactive management.

This is critical because their needs change over time.

Janitorial cleaning is ongoing in nature. It's not a one-time transaction. Clients' needs and requirements will change over time. What mattered to them two years ago or even six months ago is different to what matters to them now. Businesses change. People change in organizations too.

We want to win clients and keep them forever. We can only do this if we adapt and adjust our service to accommodate their changing needs. Their requirements and our service should always be in alignment.

We can only achieve this if we're proactive in our reporting, our communication and systematic in seeking feedback.

If you add regular auditing with advice on improving the appearance, hygiene and function of their facilities, you soon position yourself as a trusted professional who they rely on. This opens their wallets, giving you a greater portion of their facilities and maintenance spend. It makes you extremely referable.

Satisfied loyal customers don't just keep doing business with you, they buy more and refer you to others.

Clients will be ordering paper towels, toilet paper, coffee and other consumables from you. Not to mention carpet cleaning, window cleaning and other cleaning periodicals that can be very profitable to include in your business.

Get relationships right and they become the glue that sticks you and your cleaning contracts together. They protect you from competitors trying to take your business. It's like a giant moat that keeps competitors away from your clients.

Without building professional relationships like this your business will become vulnerable over time. If you don't communicate and adapt your service over time to the needs of your clients, other cleaning businesses will approach them, listen to them and offer solutions they want. You can't afford to lose touch with your clients or assume that just because you clean them according to a schedule and scope agreed to years ago, that's going to be enough to keep their loyalty.

If you become out of touch, a competitor can come in and say, "We'll solve this and that problem for you." Your clients might begin to say to themselves, "Well, my current cleaners, they've never talked to me about that. They've never asked me what's important about the service. They never chase me. I'm always chasing them. Maybe they just don't care anymore."

Don't put yourself in this situation. Don't react to complaints. Anticipate their needs first before anything ever becomes an issue. Some clients never complain. They just leave.

The number one reason customers leave is because they no longer think they matter to you. They don't feel listened to. They feel taken for granted. It's easy for this to happen too. Cleaning happens at night. No one sees the cleaners. Cleaning matters to businesses but it's not normally in the top list of their priorities. Clients could be dissatisfied with your cleaning but stay on with you because they're too busy to change cleaners. If you assume they're happy because they don't complain, you could be dead wrong.

If your interaction with clients is limited to sending them an invoice and responding only to complaints, don't be surprised if one day you're told they're changing cleaners. Don't be surprised if they tell you it's a budget issue or they've decided to take it in-house. They don't want you upset and they don't want to start an argument. You've practically ignored them, so why expect them to give you their full reason for terminating. Sometimes this is a ploy to get out of a contract. But do you really want to run a business that relies solely on contracts to stay in business? Believe me, if you hold them to the agreement and don't radically change your service in the meantime, they can't wait to see the end of the contract term. Worse still they'll let everyone know how upset they are. Don't be that business.

The key to avoiding this is consistent purposeful communication. Some clients will say they're busy and ask you not to email or call them. They'll tell you they'll let you know if there's a problem. As tempting as it is to comply, I make a point of laying down my ground rules for doing business with them and that includes providing daily cleaning reports and monthly audits for their business. Once I explain why I do it and why it's so integral to the service I provide, I don't get pushback. Even if they don't read any reports or any audits, I'm clearly communicating that I'm a professional. If there ever is an issue they know I'm proactive in my business and easily contactable.

You want to be more than just their cleaner. You want to be their trusted advisor. You want to be like a doctor. A doctor asks questions, makes an examination and diagnosis. You don't usually question their judgment. If they prescribe you medication, you take it.

A patient responds to a doctor this way because:

- They're in pain.
- The doctor has gone through years of training and qualifications.
- You are conditioned to accept their authority and expertise.
- You trust they have your best interest in mind.
- The doctor asks questions to understand your illness.
- They diagnose.
- They provide you with a treatment plan or prescription which you follow.

Now you're at a distinct disadvantage as a cleaning company. It doesn't matter how successful you are, how much money you make or how many employees you manage, as far as your clients are concerned, you're the cleaners in their mind. You lie at the bottom of the totem pole. They wouldn't pretend to educate their accountants on finance or teach their solicitors law, but they won't hesitate to offer their advice on cleaning as it's considered by most a low skill profession.

So, unlike the doctor example, they're not conditioned to accept your authority as a cleaning service provider.

You must work to earn their trust. And it takes time to become an expert in their mind. The easiest way to do this is to introduce technology and reporting to your cleaning.

This builds trust. It demonstrates that you're more than just a cleaner.

We developed our own software and an app that provided real time notifications of when the cleaners arrived, what they did, and that captured images of tasks that matter to them.

Every month an audit is sent to each client. In it, the cleaning is rated and benchmarked against our standards. In that audit we complete a compliance checklist that lists our adherence to OH&S procedures, communication procedures, and standard operating procedures. We rate our performance in areas of service that aren't directly related to the cleaning as well. And most importantly we provide suggestions and recommendations to improve the cleaning and service we provide.

What begins to happen when you do this is that you reposition yourself in their minds from being a bunch of cleaners to a team of professionals. If your recommendations are knowledgeable and useful, you start to become a trusted advisor. If you help them save money, demonstrably improve the hygiene of their workplace, and add value beyond cleaning, you'll have lifelong customers and raving fans for your business.

The secret is to make yourself indispensable.

When I was young and teaching English in Indonesia, I went for a weekend break in Pelabuhan Ratu. I was traveling by myself and stayed at a resort run by an Australian expat. Seeing me eating by myself at dinner, he invited me to his table with his friends who were also expats. I soon learnt they all had achieved success in business. In conversation, one of them placed their finger in their beer to make a big hole in their froth. This, he said, was the secret to success. Make sure if you leave your job, you'll leave a giant gap. This way you'll always be wanted and needed.

It was an interesting way of making a point, but I never forgot it. The more services and the easier and more convenient it is to do business and buy things from you, the greater the hole you create should you ever leave. If they rely on you not just for cleaning, but to stock their fridges full of milk and their cupboards with toilet paper and tissues, they'll miss this convenience if they were to change cleaners. This creates client stickiness.

Be proactive and have systems in place to build a professional relationship and value with your clients.

In short get these three fundamentals right in your business:

- A predictable quantity of profitable contracts.

- Consistent delivery of service.

- Strong client relationships.

And your business will grow profitably and sustainably every year, creating long term wealth for you and your family.

Miss any one of them and your business will be insecure and vulnerable.

Get all three legs right and your business is going to go gangbusters.

CHAPTER 10:

Hiring Staff

CHAPTER 10:
HIRING STAFF

"Coming together is a beginning. Keeping together is progress. Working together is success." – Henry Ford

So far we've covered why you'd want to own a commercial cleaning business, and the three critical elements you must have in place to win and keep profitable cleaning contracts. What we haven't yet covered is attracting, training and keeping great people to clean and grow your business.

You might not want to be 'on the tools' and even if you enjoy the physical part of the work, you can't do all the cleaning. Once you start growing your business you're going to need help.

Cleaning businesses complain about high staff turnover. It doesn't need to be this way.

Having great cleaners comes down to three things.

- Getting the right people.

- Training them right.

- Getting them to stay with you.

I don't believe you need to suffer from high staff turnover, especially in commercial cleaning. A job as a commercial cleaner will suit a lot of people because it's after hours, part time, and is a great way for them to supplement their income.

The biggest mistake I see cleaning business owners make when they're employing staff is thinking if someone has a heartbeat and a pulse that they'd be fine to fill in a cleaning position.

Cleaning is considered a low skilled menial job. There's nothing glamorous about the role and I'm yet to meet anyone whose dream is to become a cleaner – fireman, yes; doctor, yes; jet pilot, yes; a cleaner, no.

Let's not kid ourselves about the perception the public has about cleaners. The prejudice is so commonplace we might fall into the trap of thinking the same. Without thinking, we believe anyone can do the job.

You could be at a family barbecue, and you find out one of your cousins is out of work or your nephew or your friend or someone you know is looking for a job.

It's tempting to think, you've got a vacant position, you need a cleaner, why not offer them a job? You want to help and because they may be desperate for some money and some extra cash, they'll more than likely take that job.

It's unlikely they're suited to the job though. As soon as something else comes along, they're going to take it. And you've got to find someone else again.

We're talking about someone you know but the same applies when you're publicly advertising for a position, you're going to have a lot of people who aren't suited to the role, they're just looking for a stopgap between jobs.

Drawing in and attracting the right people into your business must be a priority if you want staff to stick around.

Your recruitment process isn't about getting just anyone to fill a role, it's about qualifying and weeding out unsuitable candidates.

> **PRO TIP**
>
> It's so easy to blame problems in your business on your staff. Your staff though are a reflection of your actions as a business owner.
>
> Every business gets the staff it deserves.
>
> This is why getting recruitment, training, culture and retention right are so critically important.

Have a clear picture in your mind of the type of person that is going to be suited to this role – and that's not just someone with cleaning experience. Hire on attitude. Cleaning can be taught. Attitude can't. What's the secret to having happy hardworking employees? Hire happy, hardworking people.

Some jobs will suit some personalities more than others. It makes no sense to hire a shy introvert to be in a customer service role. Likewise you wouldn't hire an outgoing personality who cares little for details to be your bookkeeper. Personality profiling is a great tool to use to determine if candidates have personalities suited to your job opening.

There are many tools and frameworks available. A simple but useful framework is DISC profiling based on the Myers–Briggs personality types.

A DISC personality assessment will give you a good guideline on determining what personalities suit different positions. It will guide you on the major personality traits, which you're going to use to choose between candidates.

DISC profiling divides people into four quadrants.

DISC divides personalities into extroverts or introverts, and task oriented or people orientated. Extroverted and task oriented individuals are 'D' type or dominant personality types – they don't make good cleaners – they're not detail oriented. They like to be in charge and be in the limelight. 'I' is for Influencers, they are people orientated extroverts – they want to talk to people – they don't care about getting a job done so as much as socializing and having fun – can you imagine how excited they'd be about cleaning night after night on their own with little to no social interaction. 'C' is for conscientious types who are task-oriented introverts – they are detail-oriented people – think engineers and accountants. Finally there are 'S' for steady types – they like routine, they don't want to rock the boat, they want to do a good job and make others happy.

I think it's pretty clear you don't want 'D's or 'I's cleaning in your business. You want 'C' s and 'S's. You want people who don't mind routine, who are conscientious and detail oriented. They don't like a lot of change.

There are short tests available for this that you can use during your interview process and I recommend you use them in addition to a short questionnaire.

Another way to qualify out candidates is to see if they can follow basic instructions. And this can be done before even they reach the interview process.

I like to put simple and specific instructions on how to respond to the job ad. The instructions are a litmus test to see whether they can follow instructions. If they can't follow simple instructions how will they go about following a cleaning scope or respond to cleaning improvement requests?

You'd be amazed how many people won't read an ad for a job they're applying for. You don't want them in your business.

And that's another key to recruiting great people. Try and make your recruitment process as close to the actual job environment as possible.

I want to give instructions that would be very similar to the instructions I might give to a cleaner, if they need to communicate onsite, get something done or do some cleaning.

So I'm going to tell them to do X, Y and Z. And in that order, if they do that, then I know they can follow instructions.

That's a big thing. You don't want someone who sees your instructions and then does something completely different. Again, don't fall into the mistake of thinking, "It's just cleaning." Anyone who can fog a mirror, who has a pulse or a heartbeat, can do the job.

You don't want those people. And if you start recruiting those people, you are going to see a high turnover of your staff.

Do you want someone with commercial cleaning experience? I would say yes but attitude always trumps experience. If they have some experience, they already know what cleaning's like and the hours involved. I don't want to hire someone who finds out in two or three weeks' time that the hours and type of work don't suit them. People with experience tend to be faster cleaners as well.

But just because they have experience, don't fall into the trap of thinking they know what they're doing.

They'll have an idea of what they're doing. They might be used to the physical nature of cleaning. That doesn't mean they're cleaning the right way or the most efficient way. You still need to train them.

They may go through the training program quicker than someone without experience, but it's not something you can skip.

Alright, so what are the steps? First we need a good job ad and it needs to attract the right candidates.

It should repel the wrong candidates.

Your ad needs to address more things than just pay and conditions. It should say why someone would want to be working for you.

What is so exciting about what you're doing as a cleaning business?

What difference are you making to customers' lives?

How do the team dynamics work?

Job applicants should be attracted and drawn to your mission and core values.

Don't think that just because you've got a paying job on offer so they should be happy and do a good job. The fact you're going to pay someone some money is not enough to attract high quality candidates.

This is not how the real world works. People are not really grateful or interested in a paycheck only.

People need to be paid, of course, and you should aim to pay them at least slightly above the standard pay rates or award rates in your state or country. But people rarely get drawn to or stay around only for money.

You need to inspire them with something more.

Cleaners should *want* to work for you, not just get a job that pays money.

All right, great, so you've got some candidates for an interview. They've got some experience, they're suited to the role. I'm going to invite them now to a live interview. And that live interview is not going to be a talking interview.

Cleaners don't get paid for talking. Cleaners, get paid for cleaning. So I want to get them into a cleaning job site environment.

I'm going to get my candidate or candidates to clean.

I pay them for this cleaning even if I don't end up hiring them, and believe me it's the best money you're going to spend on recruitment.

It's going to be a couple hours of cleaning, and you're going to find out so much information by doing this. You're going to know whether they're punctual. You're going to know what their attitude is. You're going to know what their speed is.

You're going to know if they can follow directions, whether they're clumsy, whether they can think for themselves, whether you can get along with them. So there's a whole heap of things that you're going to learn very quickly doing this.

Remember to have a checklist when assessing candidates. This way you can give each candidate a rating and a score. The higher the score the closer to the ideal candidate they should be.

By the end of this process, you'll be clear whether they're going to be suited to the job or not.

Once you've selected your candidate, you can offer them an employment contract. These contracts outline their roles, responsibilities, key performance indicators and remuneration. This contract is best prepared by a solicitor. It's important that you have restraint clauses and a condition that a confidentiality agreement is signed by your employee. You want your trade secrets to stay trade secrets, and your customers to stay your customers. The last thing you want to be doing is employing people who then decide later on they want to start their own cleaning business and take all your customers. I make sure this is given to them when I give them any formal job offer and before their job starts.

So what do you do when you hire them? Well, you've got to train them and the best way to train them is to use a training log book.

A log book tracks successful completion of tasks using the right methods and techniques. A final evaluation clean will demonstrate their knowledge, skills and readiness to clean unsupervised.

Now, every state, every country is going to be different with your legal employment obligations. All I'm going to say here is make sure that you employ people correctly and pay them right. In Australia we have the Cleaning Services Award set by Fair Work Australia. It's likely if you're not in Australia, you'll have something similar. You must pay all their employee entitlements. If you don't know how to do this, get your accountant and bookkeeper to show you. It's not hard. Don't try to take shortcuts and don't think it's easier to sham-contract – that's where you're treating an employee like they're a contractor when they really aren't. Not only could it be illegal where you operate, it's not necessary and just not worth it.

You've got to have accurate record keeping on the hours that they're doing. And there's certain obligations you're going to have in terms of having regular occupational health and safety toolbox meetings and other things.

So how do we keep good cleaners?

Keeping good cleaners is about recognition, rewards and promotion.

Hold your employees to extremely high standards but make it the best cleaning job they ever have!

Catch employees doing things right. Don't just tell them what things they're doing wrong!

Handwritten cards, gift vouchers, challenges all work. Give your employees a vision for growth and tell them how they can be promoted.

You also want to make sure your cleaners are making you money.

So, here's a few tips:

- Ease cleaners into jobs. I recommend you or your team leader work alongside them for a minimum of three months until they can work onsite without direct supervision. When they're ready, get them to do midweek cleans that require less detail, while you or your team leader does the once weekly detailed clean. You'll be faster and more detailed than them.

- Look for those cleaners who can step up and become leading hands and supervisors. Then delegate and give them more responsibility.

- Think of building teams not individual cleaners. My ideal size for small cleans is a team of three.

- Don't neglect auditing even if you think you can trust your cleaners. Remember there's a reason for the saying 'when the cats away, the mice are at play'.

- Create efficient job routing. Plan your cleaning runs.

- Create incentives for completing jobs faster while maintaining high cleaning standards. Give them vouchers even extra pay for finishing jobs faster but at the same high standard of cleaning.

- Grow your portfolio around nodes of large and small contracts. Larger jobs are great for revenue. Smaller jobs are great for profit. Get a few small jobs around the larger jobs to increase the hourly rate you make from each cleaner.

- Compare completion of tasks with allocated times per task. In other words, measure your cleaners' production rates. What gets measured gets managed.

- Recognize birthdays and celebrate wins!

There's no reason a cleaning business should suffer from high staff turnover.

But what if you really wanted to grow your cleaning business. Cleaners aren't all you need. You need a sales team.

Recruiting a sales team is going to follow a similar process to what you would follow to find cleaners. What's different is the role description and personality. And instead of trialing them with a day of cleaning, I want to trial them with a day of prospecting and sales.

In general, you want a 'D' or 'I' personality for sales. I want someone who's competitive and goal orientated. At the same time I'm looking for someone who can follow a system and is happy working with a consistent routine.

In later chapters I'm going to cover franchising a cleaning business. If you franchise out a cleaning business you won't have to hire cleaners. Your franchisees will be doing that. Instead, you'll want to hire salespeople. A sales team will be critical if you want to double, triple or achieve ten times your growth.

It is possible to run a cleaning business without any staff but you'll be imposing limits on the work you can take on. And it's definitely possible to run a master franchise without employees and without cleaning staff. But if size and growth are important to you, you need people.

CHAPTER 11:
Mistakes and Misconceptions

CHAPTER 11:
MISTAKES AND
MISCONCEPTIONS

"The trouble with the world is not that they know too little; it's that they know too many things that just aren't so." – Mark Twain

We're almost ready to cover franchising a commercial cleaning business. This book, though, wouldn't be complete if I didn't include a list of mistakes to avoid and misconceptions that could set you back years, maybe even completely derail you in your cleaning entrepreneurial journey.

Thinking Success Will Happen Overnight

There is no substitute for persistence and consistent action. Cleaning contracts take time to accumulate. You must allow for a sales cycle. When you start, it can test your commitment and resolve. If you start sending proposals, nothing much will happen in the first few weeks. You'll start to wonder if this works. At this point, it's tempting to give up. Don't! Napoleon Hill in his famous book *Think and Grow Rich* wrote a chapter entitled 'Three Feet from Gold'. He wrote the story of a man who gave up on a mine three feet shy of a gold strike! Don't make the same mistake! You must allow the process some time. It can take up to eight weeks before you see consistent results from your activity. But once the deals flow, they come thick and fast!

The dollar value of your initial deals may be lower at the start too. Most people start by winning smaller deals worth $150 to $350 per month.

Larger contracts typically take more time to win. Contracts that pay $10,000 a month or more take longer to win than $1000 per month contracts.

You've got to allow time and consistent action to work before you start seeing results. And when the contracts start flowing, don't stop. Momentum is your friend. If you stop, you'll need to build your pipeline all over again.

Stopping and starting a cleaning contract sales pipeline all the time will dramatically slow down your progress in contract acquisition.

Consistency wins!

A cleaning business is built by adding contracts consistently. This takes time. The time it takes will depend on your income goals and the amount of work you put into cleaning contract acquisition.

And it's not just winning contracts that require consistency. Keeping customers and leading people means communicating and showing up every day.

Doing It Alone - and Ruling Out Franchising Completely

For a relatively small investment, franchises give you access to systems and tools proven to work and that often have taken years and sometimes millions of dollars to develop. The good ones provide support and guidance to help you achieve the level of success you're aiming for.

Franchise systems though are not made equal.

When I started, I looked at buying a franchise first. Why? Because I saw no reason to reinvent the wheel. It seemed smarter to me to work hard and be confident of the returns on my effort, than experiment and fail. I wanted to fast-track my business and buying a franchise made sense.

The reason I didn't invest in a franchise in the end was not because of the initial outlay or fees. In most franchises these are reasonable. The reason I didn't join a franchise was because none of the janitorial franchise systems I spoke with were interested in showing me how to win contracts, employ a team or grow my business. Their models were to sell contracts to me so that I would clean myself. Beyond that very little support or guidance was provided. Some of them even told me I wasn't meant to speak with my clients as they would do that for me.

I wasn't interested in buying a cleaning job. I wanted a business.

If you're reading this book and have gotten this far, I'm guessing you want a business too, not a job. When researching franchises, find out what tools and resources are available to grow your business. Are you treated as a business owner or merely a cleaner? Do they provide programs and support to win contracts, manage staff and expand your business. If they don't or it's not the primary focus to equip their franchises with the tools and support to manage their own business, odds on, you're just buying a job.

You might be thinking, "Maybe I'll just go and buy some cleaning contracts," or, "I'll buy some equipment and land some cleaning contracts. It seems like it's pretty easy to do." It's true when you know how, this is more than achievable, but learning how is difficult. I invested hundreds and hundreds of thousands of dollars learning how to do it. I've had sales teams experiment with different scripts. I've experimented with countless marketing channels and methods. Some work, some don't. Some work but are too time-consuming and costly to be viable.

If your ambition is to run a national cleaning company making hundreds of millions of dollars a year, it might not make sense to invest in a franchise unless it's a master franchise. If on the other hand, you're looking at making a few hundred thousand a year or a few million, investing in a good franchise is often the fastest and most reliable way of getting there.

If you try and do it yourself, you're bound to make mistakes. I did. I made countless in fact. It took me a long time before I really worked it out and by that stage I had reinvested millions in development. Working it out yourself is possible, but it's just risky and slow. Things aren't proven. Maybe your ideas will work, maybe they won't. There's a lot of unknowns. The benefit of investing in a proven franchise system is that you have a proven predictable system you can follow. There's a known process. If you put the investment and hard work in, you know that you're going to get some returns.

It ended up taking me years to work out how to win business, and in the first couple years I earned less than $50,000. It was slow going. Had I bought the right franchise I would have made a lot more money. And it was time that ended up being my biggest cost.

When it became my time to franchise the business I had created, I was determined to create an opportunity for any one of our franchise owners to grow their business and win their own contracts.

My experience highlights a couple points:

- Choosing the right franchise is more important than choosing to buy a franchise or not.

- You've got to be clear on your goals and honest about your skills before deciding on a franchise. Franchise systems are different even in commercial cleaning. Not all of them will suit you or help you achieve your goals

Let's cover the reasons for and against buying a franchise.

Before we talk about the pros of investing in a franchise, let's talk about the cons and the wrong reasons to buy into a franchise.

Buying a franchise is a bad idea if you want to do things only your way. This kind of defeats the purpose of buying a franchise because it's a system that you're looking at buying. But if you just want a brand name and some cleaning contracts but are going to do things your way, it's going to be a miserable experience for you and your franchisor.

Don't buy a franchise if you think it will guarantee your success. It doesn't matter how good a franchise system is – you could buy a McDonald's or a Ford dealership, franchises you might think guarantee success – but if you don't put in the work or you're not suited to run the business with your skillset, it won't work. No one can guarantee your success except yourself!

The third reason not to buy a franchise is related to the second and that's thinking a franchise is a passive investment – thinking all you need to do is put the money in, and the system will take care of the rest. That is a fantasy business. You've got to put work in no matter whether you buy a franchise or go independent.

Franchises also have fees and royalties. This is perhaps the biggest reason people object to buying a franchise. There are people who jump up and down, saying you shouldn't buy a franchise because of the fees. All you need is a website, an eBook and some cleaning gear, they say.

In a franchise you are also going to have some restrictions around what you can or can't do running your business. You don't get to decide on brand colors. You might be limited in what you can experiment with or try. You'll have to follow a manual of operations.

And finally, you'll have geographic limitations. You won't be able to grow nationally or internationally without buying additional territories or getting permission from your franchisor.

We've covered the cons, what are the pros?

-   You get years of knowhow, and a recipe proven to work. What this means is you can save years and shortcut your way to money and profit. Your franchise fee gives you access to all the intellectual property at a significant discount to the amount of money it would cost you to develop anything close to the equivalent. You get to remove all the trial and error from getting started.

-   If the franchise has developed a brand and spent time creating a strong unique selling point (USP) for their business, you can charge higher prices for the cleaning than you could as an unknown startup. This should more than cover any royalties or service fees.

-   You get support. You're in business for yourself but not by yourself.

-   Cleaning contracts can be won for you in systems like Urban Clean. You are effectively outsourcing sales. This can be much cheaper than hiring or training a salesperson to do this function for you, especially if you have limited experience in sales or managing sales teams. And best of all you pay only when a contract is won for you. In Urban Clean's system for instance you can pay that money over time which means customers are cash flowing your contract acquisition costs.

Let's talk about some misconceptions around franchising. The first is that all franchises in an industry are more or less the same. The only difference is their fee structure.

The truth is low fees doesn't necessarily equal a great franchise.

What's better: 10% royalty at $20 per hour or 20% at $100 per hour? A 5% fee on $20,000 or a 15% fee on $500,000?

Questions you want to ask are:

- Does the franchisor teach you how to win your own accounts or are you reliant only on the business they give you?

- Does the fee structure stay the same as you grow the business or is it fixed no matter your size?

- Do you get shown how to recruit, run and manage teams or are you expected to always do the cleaning?

- Does the franchise position itself as a premium cleaning option that commands above market prices? Or does it compete mostly on price?

Some cleaning franchises are more focused on cleaning, some more on operations, some more on management, others more on sales. Just because the industry is the same doesn't mean the opportunity or the business is operated the same way in every franchise system.

PRO TIP

Be careful of your prejudices.

Even I carried some prejudices against franchising until I understood that franchising was only a business model designed for duplication and support.

Not all franchises are the same.

Franchise systems can be radically different from each other even in the same industry.

Even in the same franchise system there will be different opportunities. Urban Clean for example has Unit Franchises and Master Franchises.

Unit franchises will be more hands-on, working directly with clients and managing cleaning teams. Our Master Franchises on the other hand don't clean or manage cleaning teams, their business is focused on sales and coaching.

Another misconception is that service fees or royalties is dead money. In fact, if you're working with the right franchise system it's the best money that you will ever invest running a business.

Think of your electricity, utilities or phone bill. Does your phone company or electricity company care whether you stay in business or not?

When you've put petrol in your car, does the oil company care whether your business stays afloat or not? Maybe at a macro level they do, but as an individual business you mean nothing to them.

Your landlord might care more that you stay around in business, but they can't coach you or support you directly in the sales and performance of your business.

When you pay service fees or royalties you get direct support to help you run your business and you have a business partner – your franchisor – that has a vested interest in your success.

You're in business for yourself, but not by yourself.

Your franchisor wants to see you succeed. They can jump in and actually help you turn around your business if you're facing challenges, or if you want to get even bigger they can help you to accelerate growth.

Because your success is their success.

Service fees are one of the best investments that you could ever make in a business when you find the right partner to be working with.

'Bright Shiny Object' Syndrome

This is a disease all entrepreneurs are vulnerable to. We look for the easy and fast option. So when things get tough or slow, and at some time that is going to happen as business owners, we're tempted to look for quick fixes and better shinier options.

With so much information available to us and so many ideas circulating this can be an irresistible temptation. We see people making fortunes in property, Amazon reselling, cryptocurrencies or NFTs. We think that could be me, that looks easy. If you succumb to this temptation, your focus will be split and dissipated. When attention and focus are divided, progress and results slow.

If you do jump across to a new bright shiny object, it's not long before you discover that to succeed takes just as much time and energy as what you were doing before.

Overnight successes are years in the making. There are no silver bullets either. Time, work, and consistent action are what bring about results. There will be setbacks. Sometimes progress will be slow. It will take time. The secret to success is this: follow a plan, and see it through. Then keep doing it.

Thinking One Big Contract Will Solve Everything

There are some big contracts in janitorial cleaning. You might know somebody who's had a commercial cleaning contract or had a commercial cleaning business and they might tell you about this one big contract that they've got. They may have a contract for a shopping mall, or stadium and it seems they're making so much money. Well, I can tell you now that the big contracts are not where this game is won. That is short-term thinking.

People can boast about their contracts but it's profits that matter and it's actually a lot of the smaller stuff that brings in the bacon.

And profit margins aren't the only problem. Having only a few large accounts means your business is at risk should you lose any one account. I learnt this the hard way. Don't make any account more than 10% of your business. Better still don't make any single account more than 1%. It makes for better sleep!

It's Okay to Have No Systems

There's a lot more to running a cleaning business than cleaning. Yes, cleaning is what's done, but it's the systems behind the cleaning that make or break a cleaning business. You want to be able to grow and scale and build teams. This is impossible without the right operational, training and recruiting systems.

You want more profitable cleaning contracts when you want them. You need an effective sales and marketing system.

You want customers to stay and spend more money with you. You need a customer retention and engagement system.

Ultimately, businesses work or don't work because of systems or the lack of them. Without systems businesses are run on the fly. Growth is unpredictable and you'll be forever complaining you can't find good people. People won't be the problem in this case. The problem is that everyone has to make things up as they go. There are no tried and proven steps to follow. And this won't be the fault of the staff and employees of the business. It'll be yours because you have no systems.

Reinventing the Wheel

Your problems are not so unique that no one's ever had to face them before. Like King Solomon said "There's nothing new under the sun."

And if other people have faced them, other people have solved them. Why reinvent the wheel?

The fastest way to success is to follow someone else's success.

If you try and do it yourself, you're bound to make mistakes, wasting a lot of time and money. Hey, I did. I made a ton of mistakes. It took me a long time before I really worked this thing out and I had to invest a lot of money to do this. There was a lot of guesswork and a lot of blind alleyways that went nowhere.

Things weren't proven. There were a lot of unknowns. I put hard work in, I put a lot of money in, but the outcomes were mostly unknown. The benefit of joining a franchised system with an established system that you know works is that things become predictable, they're proven, there's systems and there's results that you can follow. Once it's a known process, you put the hard work in, put the investment in, knowing the chance of getting good returns is high.

On my journey I had some close calls and lucky breaks and some great people around me. It could have easily been otherwise.

CHAPTER 12:

The Secret to Winning

CHAPTER 12:
THE SECRET TO WINNING

"Attitude is a little thing that makes a big difference." – *Winston Churchill*

In this chapter I'm going to share with you one key without which you have no chance of winning in business.

I don't care how little you know today, what setbacks you've had or what mistakes you've made in the past – if you have a great attitude you will succeed and you will achieve great things.

Bad things happen. If there's one thing I'm sure of, I'm sure of this, things won't always go your way. You will have setbacks. How we meet and overcome those setbacks will determine in large part your level of success in this business.

It's what separates winners from losers.

Before we get into what attitude you need to have to succeed, let's start by defining what we mean by attitude and success.

These words get thrown around so much that they have become almost meaningless.

I define attitude as the angle you approach business, the angle for that matter you approach life. Your thinking, your beliefs, the questions you ask yourself and how you're inclined to act are what define your attitude. It's how you are prepared to meet situations in life and how you go after things you want.

Attitude was a vague term to me until I learnt how to fly a plane.

Attitude means something very specific when flying a plane. If you put your plane in the wrong attitude and don't correct that attitude, you will stall, lose control of your plane and die! Attitude is not a wishy-washy concept in aviation! It's a matter of life and death.

Your attitude is defined as the position of your plane in relation to the horizon. Piloting a plane is a matter of putting the plane in the correct attitude and applying the right amount of power.

One of the surprising things I found out when learning to fly is that when you come in to land, you don't use power to go faster or slower. You use power to adjust your height and your pitch or attitude to adjust speed. The higher you angle or pitch the plane up, the slower you fly. The lower you pitch down the nose, the faster you go.

You can fly with the right power settings but if your attitude is wrong this could mean a bumpy landing or much worse.

We've covered the meaning of attitude, so what's success?

What does it mean to succeed?

If we look up 'succeed' in the dictionary we find its meaning is derived from its Latin origins 'sub cedere' – to yield under. To succeed is to have something fall under you. Your efforts yield to you your goal, you achieve your objective. This could be a position, a battle, or winning a game.

Basically 'success' means getting what you want.

That means you need to have a clear goal in mind. Don't have a nebulous wish or vague desire like 'I want to make more money'. That could be one dollar more. Get specific. How many new cleaning contracts do you want, what revenue do you want to be making, what profit? How much extra time for your family? Have a specific number as a target.

I mean, how will you know when you've succeeded if you don't know what success even is? It seems so straightforward when you say it like that but it's amazing how many people want success but don't even know what success looks like to them. They have no target they are aiming for.

To succeed you need a goal and to work a plan that has a high chance of success. And by the way this is why people invest in a franchise.

We've defined attitude. We've defined success.

So what's the right attitude to take if we want to achieve a new level of income or customer satisfaction in your cleaning business?

In Urban Clean, we created a set of core principles that we call our rules of the game. We follow these rules when we run our business.

To help remember them we've used each letter of URBAN to stand for a rule.

Unparalleled – We learn and share from each other's mistakes and successes for the benefit of everyone in Urban Clean.

Responsibility – We live above the line.

Be a Team – We get along to get the job done.

Action – We are action takers.

No compromise – We are obsessed about delivering a consistently positive customer experience.

These are all critical to growing and developing as an organization, but one in particular is essential for individual achievement and that's R for Responsibility. We live above the line. It's an attitude and approach we take to everything we do in business.

What's above the line?

If you haven't come across this concept before, 'above or below the line' is about two modes or two attitudes towards life. One moves us closer to our goals, the other prevents us from reaching them at all.

Above the line is defined by

- Ownership
- Accountability
- Responsibility

Did you notice ownership accountability and responsibility start with the letters O A R – oar – this makes it easier to remember because an oar is a tool you use to get to where you want to go.

A below the line attitude is characterized by

- Blame
- Excuse
- Denial

PRO TIP

The day you take full accountability and ownership for the results in your personal life and in your business life is the day your life transforms.

It's the difference between being a child and becoming an adult.

Blame, excuses and denial start with the letters BED – bed – this is something passive. You lie down. You give up control. You externalize all your results. Things happen to you and there's nothing you can do about them. You think life would only get better if other people were better or bad things didn't happen to you. There's no two ways about it, this is a loser's attitude.

So that's the concept. So how does this play out running a cleaning business?

Let's consider a real-life example.

You get a difficult customer. They're picky, they complain all the time, and nothing seems ever good enough for them.

If we take a 'below the line' attitude, we might be defensive. We might deny that anything's wrong. We might think straight away the customer is being unreasonable and being a pain in the backside. Or you might just tolerate it as something okay to have in your business, or make excuses saying that it's your staff not you. All that complaining, blaming, excuse making and denial results in NOTHING. It doesn't change the situation. You're just going to get angry, frustrated and upset. And that's it.

You're waiting around hoping the situation will get better by itself. I got news for you. It won't. This attitude is no better than planning your retirement on winning the lottery. It could happen, but don't count on it.

An 'above the line' attitude would be characterized by being responsible, taking ownership of the situation, and a willingness to be accountable for results and outcomes. You could ask yourself, how do I address the underlying issue that's getting me all these complaints? Can I create a system or follow a system I already have that I may not be following? Can I work with my customer to agree on a standard? Do I need to change pricing or the scope of work with my customer? Or is this customer just plain nuts and I need to learn how to win more accounts so I can let them go?

You're taking a problem-solving attitude now and it's obvious with this attitude that you are going to move your business forward. You'll work it out with the customer. You'll fix any problems with your service. You may even end up raising your prices or get new profitable business to replace the account.

Good things happen with this attitude.

I used the case of a difficult customer, but you can apply it to not reaching sales targets, dealing with difficult employees, losing an account – you name it.

You take an above the line attitude when you take action, you ask questions, you learn, seek solutions, be open, you work with others, you ask yourself how you can do better, how can you improve the situation.

And here's a big one: you educate yourself on cleaning and business. You search things on Google, read books, use the resources around you. If you're part of a developed franchise they'll have manuals and systems. I'll tell you a sad truth. I'm a franchisor and we've put years of knowledge and knowhow into our manuals and yet I still have a handful of franchisees who only ever looked at them at the start of their training.

One indicator that you do in fact have an above the line attitude is that you're reading this book!

So, kudos to you.

You take a 'below the line' attitude when you wait for others or point fingers at others.

You think and say things like, "This happened because such and such happened... I can't because... xyz. If they hadn't done this, I wouldn't have done that... Easy for them to say... Or why does this always happen to me." Or you could ignore the situation and pretend there's no problem or say that's got nothing to do with you because that's somebody else's job. You stay stuck in a problem.

Nothing good comes from a 'below the line' attitude.

Having an 'above the line' attitude is the number one deciding factor in your success in this industry, and for that matter, anything in life.

Let me share with you a tip to turn any setback into fuel for your success.

When I hit rock bottom in my real estate development business, I had to start over again with next to nothing. At first, I was depressed and demoralized. One day I opened my mailbox to find a letter. It was a letter from a solicitor. I had been sent a claim saying I owed someone over $100,000. I couldn't believe it. I was upset. I was angry. It was a spurious baseless claim, but they were threatening me with legal action.

This was a lot of money to me then. I had lost everything at this stage except the family home and my wife was pregnant with our second child. If this claim was successful, the prospect of losing the little we still had was real.

One night I was standing on my balcony staring out to the city like I was staring out into the abyss when it struck me – I had no control over this claim. I could be worried, upset, and complain about it but it was something outside of my control. I was worried and upset because $100,000 meant a lot of money to me. I thought if I was Richard Branson or Bill Gates would I care about this sum? Of course not. Their resources were much bigger than the problem I had. 100k would be a drop in the ocean to them.

I realized at that moment I couldn't control the problem or the size of the problem, but I could control if I let that problem stay big or become small to me. So, I resolved to work to a point where $100,000 was not a huge amount to me. Win or lose the legal case, it would not mean I would lose our family home.

This was the initial fuel I used to start a commercial cleaning business and grow it into a multimillion-dollar enterprise.

I learnt later Jim Rohn was famous for saying "don't wish life was easier, wish that you were better".

Problems will always exist. The question is, will the problem be bigger, the same size, or smaller than you?

I was fortunate the claim proved to be baseless and went nowhere. But I'm forever grateful for the experience because it taught me to become bigger than my problems.

The right attitude makes all the difference. Whatever challenge or obstacle you come across; you can still win if you face it with the right attitude.

CHAPTER 13:
Stages of a Janitorial Business

CHAPTER 13:
STAGES OF A JANITORIAL BUSINESS

"A big business starts small." – Richard Branson

In this chapter I'm going to talk about franchising a commercial cleaning business. And what I mean by franchising is converting a cleaning business into a franchised operation that recruits franchisees who operate their own cleaning business.

I'll be covering why you'd want to franchise a cleaning business and why running a traditional cleaning business can be so hard after about a million in revenue. And what steps you need to take if you are looking at franchising a cleaning business.

Before you even consider franchising a cleaning business, you've got to have worked out two fundamentals that we've already covered:

- How to win cleaning contracts and how to do that consistently, predictably and profitably.

- How to keep those cleaning contracts.

It's a rare cleaning business that's worked out both. But let's assume you've got both of these fundamentals worked out in your business.

The question is, then, if you know how to win cleaning contracts, and you can keep them, why would you bother franchising your business?

You could just get staff and keep on winning cleaning contracts, right?

Well, in a sense you're right and it's exactly the business a unit franchisee wants and buys into. And there is no need to consider franchising out your business if you plan on turning over less than a million a year in cleaning contracts.

At this size, a cleaning business is manageable. You can directly oversee the cleaning, manage staff, liaise with clients. It can be a profitable little business. It is going to involve hands-on management. It's likely you would be hands-on or at least supervising your cleaners. You would be training and hiring your staff, inspecting sites for quality control, rostering shifts and communicating on a daily basis with your clients.

Once you reach about a million in revenue, even if you're not hands-on with the cleaning, you'll have a full-time job looking after the non-cleaning parts of the business.

It's at this point the business becomes difficult if you want to continue to grow. If you want to grow the business, someone has to go out and quote for cleaning contracts. If this is not you, you're hiring someone unless you don't mind growing slowly. Remember, you're already stretched with the operational and administrative tasks of the business. Fitting a quote in here or there is about all you can do.

PRO TIP

All businesses have natural plateaus.

To break through them requires a different business model and way of operating.

If you choose to do the selling full-time, you need to hire someone to take over the operational and administrative roles. So you're going to lose profit margin as soon as you decide you want to grow the business.

It gets worse. If you win a contract, you'll need to use your existing income or external funds to start the account. Commercial cleaning is account-based cleaning. Clients typically pay monthly accounts 30 to 60 days from the end of the month. This means you'll need to cover overheads, equipment and cleaners' salaries for up to 60 or 90 days before payment. Now there are ways to reduce this payment gap or finance it, but it will always exist in a commercial cleaning business.

This starts a negative cash flow cycle.

You decide to grow. You hire sales or management staff. You lose profit immediately by doing so. You then win contracts. You now need to find money to fund the startup costs of these new accounts. This is a sunk cost that you won't see back until you finish the contract. Let's say you win a $10,000 per month account that is won at a 20% gross margin. Technically you're making $2000 a month profit from them. But if that client doesn't pay for 60 days, you'll need to outlay $16,000 before that account starts paying for itself. It will take another ten months before you get that money back and start making money.

It doesn't end there because as you grow, you'll need a diverse management team. Someone who trains your cleaners, then someone who takes care of invoicing and accounts, an account manager, a supervisor and salespeople. All this was manageable when the business was small and you took on these tasks yourself. Even if you weren't skilled at one of these tasks, your passion and enthusiasm as the business owner was enough to get you through. You can't expect the same from employees. Buying a franchise that provides support and systems for these functions of the business will alleviate but never eradicate these challenges.

And this all assumes you know what you're doing, you have high client retention rates, and every part of your business is systemized and documented. That does not describe the majority of businesses turning over less than $1 million in revenue.

It's not until a cleaning business passes between $3–5 million dollars that it has enough infrastructure to continue growing at a steady pace while still making profit for the owner.

Because of the cash flow constraints, I call the journey between $1 million and $3 million in revenue, the cleaning business valley of death. Most never get to the other side. And without outside capital it is near impossible without a 10-to-20-year horizon. Even once you've passed $3 million in revenue, the rate of your growth will always be constrained by access to capital to start new accounts.

When cleaning businesses hit this ceiling, and it can happen when the revenue hits as little as $300,000 right up to $3 million a year – depending on the types of accounts the business has – a lot of cleaning businesses decide it makes more sense to stay small than to go broke getting big.

I just described a stock standard traditional commercial cleaning business.

And it's for this reason, franchising out a commercial cleaning business is so attractive.

Instead of it costing you to grow, people will be paying you to grow the business.

A master franchise, if set up correctly, is not going to face the cash flow and growth challenges of a typical cleaning business.

Franchising a cleaning business will give you these immediate advantages:

- You're going to recruit franchises who give you tens of thousands of dollars and sometimes hundreds of thousands of dollars to get set up in their business.

- Your franchisees will be paying you money when you win contracts.

- You're be building a residual income stream from these contracts as you're going to receive a percentage of all their income

- You can keep winning and selling contracts for them without worrying about cash flow

- They're the ones who are going to manage client relationships and their cleaning teams so operational infrastructure is not necessary

Staff, in this model, are completely optional. You are not responsible for cleaner salaries, supervisors or account managers. Your franchisees clean themselves, or employ, train and manage their own cleaners. They liaise and communicate with their clients.

Cash flow is not a problem when you win an account. In fact, you'll be <u>paid</u> money when you win accounts. And because franchisees aren't employees or subcontractors, they get paid when their clients pay them. You are not responsible for their payments. You don't need to buy machinery and cleaning equipment. Your franchisees will do that.

What this means for you is that you can get on with growing and building a business, winning more cleaning contracts without worrying that you'll grow faster than your cash flow allows. You have leverage in this business model and get to benefit from OPM and OPT – other people's money and other people's time.

In fact, a master franchise in commercial cleaning ticks the three big boxes we want from any business, capital, cash flow and residual income streams. All businesses will have at least one income stream, some have two, but it's rare for a business to have all three. Capital is received from franchise sales, cash flow from the sale of cleaning contracts, and residual income from the percentage of cleaning contract income you receive from your franchisees. The operational costs can be minimal too as your franchisees outlay capital and wages to service the clients you win for them.

It could almost be said this is the perfect business.

It seemed so to me, so I set about documenting and packaging up my business into a ready-made system that could be sold as a franchise.

In the next chapter I'll tell you how I did it.

CHAPTER 14:
Franchising a Cleaning Business

CHAPTER 14:
FRANCHISING A CLEANING BUSINESS

"The more I help others succeed, the more I succeed." – Ray Kroc

In an earlier chapter, I recounted how selling a handful of cleaning contracts made me aware of just how many people wanted to buy cleaning contracts and start their own business. I had worked out how to win accounts at higher-than-average market rates, so I knew that even if I charged a reasonable ongoing fee for use of the systems and support, a potential franchisee would still be receiving much more money than if they operated independently.

There was no question a franchisee was getting value when they invested with me.

The biggest challenge for new business owners is sales. I removed this problem by winning business for new franchisees starting in their business. At first, I offered all franchises with pre-existing cleaning contracts which gave them immediate income.

Selling a franchise couldn't be hard then?

I listed my newly minted franchise on business listings and waited for the phone to ring. The phone did ring. When I spoke to prospective franchisees, my conversations followed a similar pattern to the ones I had before I franchised and was selling a handful of cleaning accounts. I talked about what contracts I could sell with the franchise and then explained all the benefits of buying the franchise. They asked me a bunch of questions normally related to franchise fees, and how many hours they would have to work for the cleaning contract income. I did my best to answer their questions and sell them the opportunity.

This went on for months.

Still, I hadn't recruited a franchise. First, I thought I must be struggling because I wasn't a known brand. But this didn't explain how others had got franchise systems up and running. At one point, they weren't known brands either.

Success leaves clues. So I started talking to other franchisors and reading their books. This is when I came across Jim Penman's book, *Selling by Not Selling*. In it, Penman talked about how he faced the exact same problem I was having.

Before he franchised his lawn mowing business, he would sell lawn mowing rounds. To sell them he would talk about how great the round was, how much money people could make and so on. He sold them but it was a hard slog. On one occasion, he spoke to someone who had no idea how to start a mowing business. Instead of selling the round, Penman took time to explain how to get started, what equipment he needed and how to grow a mowing round. The guy was shopping around for a mowing business, and told Penman he was still talking to others. Later, Penman got a call back from him and told Penman he'd buy his mowing round. It turned out he didn't have the best deal in terms of the numbers, but Penman had won his trust by sharing his knowledge. This was selling by not selling.

I realized then, I wasn't educating prospective franchisees, I was pitching them.

I radically changed my approach to recruiting prospective franchisees. My job became to educate them on how to run a successful commercial cleaning business. This allowed me to build trust with them and demonstrate my expertise.

I was now having more in-depth conversations with them and getting much more engagement from candidates, but that still wasn't enough to get people to make a commitment. Most were reluctant to be the first ever franchisee with me.

People liked what they heard from me. They liked the opportunity in theory. What they wanted was proof they would get a return on their investment. So I started showing them the jobs at night I had that could become their accounts. I got them to speak with my cleaners who told them exactly how long jobs took them to clean.

People liked this but they wanted more.

They wanted GUARANTEES!

It seemed crazy. I was giving them cleaning contracts. Shouldn't that be enough?

A breakthrough happened when I guaranteed their contract value if they lost it through no fault of their own. This was enough to get my first franchisee across the line.

I had a number of calls and meetings with them and had shown them the jobs available. Since I was still operating from my garage at the time, we met in a cafe to fill in the application form. I remember taking their franchise application form to the print shop to get a photocopy made for them. It was the proudest walk I had ever made in a shopping center.

My method of recruitment relied on having cleaning contracts always ready and available for new franchises. This meant I always had to run a cleaning business with cleaners. It also meant my business was constrained by the speed I could acquire business and since I had to incur the costs of acquiring and servicing those accounts before franchises were sold. This put a strain on my cash flow and limited my growth.

The solution was to offer a guarantee that terrified me. Instead of having contracts always ready for new franchisees before they started, I guaranteed to give their money back if I couldn't win their contract value within four months. This was going to be a stretch for me back then especially if I recruited more than two franchisees a month.

In the first year, I recruited only five franchisees. In the second year of franchising, I introduced the moneyback guarantee and in that year I recruited 21 franchisees. I only had to return someone's money twice. The pressure to get cleaning contracts predictably and fast led to many of the breakthroughs in cleaning contract acquisition and marketing I've covered earlier in this book. Because the methods I had to develop to win contracts were so predictable, we got to the point where we needed only to guarantee the activity necessary to get them their initial value of contracts. And there's no question that now having a brand and a proven track record makes recruiting franchisees far easier.

I learnt over this time that it was one thing to recruit a franchise and another thing to develop them as business owners. The more money my franchisees made, the more money I made. I had to develop tools, systems and methods of support so they could not only retain clients but have the capacity to win and take on new clients and grow their business profitably.

PRO TIP

Some cleaning businesses franchise their operations and find they're unable to recruit more than 20 or 30 franchisees.

This is normally the case when the fundamentals such as acquisition of clients and operations are not systemized and duplicatable.

It can also happen when the model isn't profitable for both the franchisees and the franchisor.

I wanted them to have the skills to manage cleaning teams of their own and run a profitable business. This allowed me to sell more cleaning contracts to them or get a percentage of the cleaning contracts they were winning on their own using the system I'd developed. And of course, if they did well, they would say good things about the system when prospective franchisees called them.

So How Do You Build Such a System?

You are going to need three things to make this happen

1. A predictable method of acquiring profitable cleaning contracts at volume.

2. A way to package this up as a highly attractive 'ready-made' business.

3. A scalable, manageable system for support and growth of your franchisees.

We've covered in earlier chapters how to win contracts predictably and at high dollar values. The steps involve:

- Identifying your most profitable target market namely, what is the most profitable segment in the industry and what does that customer look like?

- Identifying your target market's list of needs.

- Articulating needs. They might say they want one thing but they really want something else more important to them. The market is a genius and moron at the same time. Henry Ford famously said on this that "If I asked people what they wanted, they would have told me a faster horse."

- Designing solutions around those articulated needs and crystallizing an offer and service.

- Creating a sales system that demonstrates undeniably that you deliver these solutions. This is the difference between showing a packet of Oreos as opposed to cookies and cream biscuits in a brown paper bag. Providing guarantees, proof, and demonstrating your service outcomes are part of this.

- Having a cost-effective, activity-based marketing method that predictably builds a pipeline that converts into sales. This is the Quick Connect Method that gets as many proposals as you want and builds a database for you at the same time.

- Creating a quoting system, CRM and a sales dashboard.

Next you've got to package this up as a highly attractive 'ready-made' business.

The first step in this is to prepare your franchise documentation. In your franchise documents you will include all your terms, fees, conditions, protections and minimum performance criteria. You need to have an understanding of what the market will accept and what fees are required to make the business feasible whilst giving franchisees a strong return on investment.

The key is to make it fair for everyone and incentivize franchisees that want to grow their business.

Be clear on what's not accepted in the business and the consequences of not achieving minimum benchmarks and standards.

Next is to have a reliable and cost-effective means of marketing the franchise opportunity. If you have the right offer and proof of franchisee success this won't be a problem.

Demonstrate undeniably that you can win contracts. This means not only showing a track record, it includes showing your sales process and why it gets the results it does.

If you guarantee you can do this, franchisees will pay you upfront for winning them contracts before you've secured any cleaning account.

In fact, if you unpack the method to win the cleaning contracts, you can guarantee the activity to get those results not the results themselves. This is important because if all you did is just show them that you've got some cleaning contracts ready to go that they can buy, it's not going to convince many people to buy a franchise from you. I made this mistake when first recruiting franchises. You will scare good prospects away. Good prospects want to know there's a predictable way for them to grow their business. This is a big reason for them to buy a franchise instead of an established independent business. They want to know you can win more for them or that you can show them how to win them for themselves.

Even though their contracts may not be available to them straight away, they know they're coming and they know that they can then grow their business using the same method you use to win them their initial contracts.

When you can do this and demonstrate this undeniably to them, they will pay you upfront before you've got any contracts at all.

The recruitment process is an educational journey not a sales pitch. This builds trust. It demonstrates your expertise and shows that you care. People want to do business with you when you're happy to reveal to them exactly what's required in order to operate a successful commercial cleaning business.

Finally design a 'set-up and then support' model where new franchisees take on full responsibility for operating their business.

This last step is about giving franchisees freedom to grow the business on their own and giving you time freedom. You don't want to be the middle person between clients and your franchisees. You don't want to be managing the business for them and you want some of them to be expanding their business on their own. Leave micromanaging to the psychopaths!

What we're talking about is a scalable, manageable system for growth and support.

This will come down to:

- Creating a selection-criteria for prospective franchisees.

- Having online training manuals and procedures.

- Giving franchisees easy to use tools and processes.

- Having an effective training and onboarding program.

- Nurturing a culture of responsibility – blame, excuses and denial should not be normal.

- Creating streamlined processes, forms and scalable support – you want to get to the point where the systems of support are so good, 15 minute monthly coaching sessions work once a franchisee is established in their business.

- Having an Integrated Management System for constant improvement and feedback loops. This allows for continuous ongoing improvement.

You now have a formula for franchising success.

CHAPTER 15:

Creating the Right Franchise Offer

CHAPTER 15:
CREATING THE RIGHT
FRANCHISE OFFER

"If you give a man a fish, you feed him for a day. If you teach a man to fish, you feed him for a lifetime." – African proverb

In the last chapter, I outlined the steps needed to franchise a cleaning business.

I'm going to be honest though. If you're looking at doing this yourself, you're looking at a minimum two-year process, and minimum spend of $500,000 getting it right, and that's if you've already got the fundamentals worked out and have expertise in franchising. It took me much longer and I spent a lot more money getting it right.

When I first started, I made one big mistake. I relied on just having cleaning contracts. I had cleaning contracts and with those cleaning contracts, I thought, "Oh, great. I'll put up these contracts for sale with a franchise. That will be enough for people to want to buy and with ongoing fees I'll support them in their business."

It's not as simple as that. What I ended up doing is attracting the wrong people into the business. I struggled not just to sell it as a franchise, I wasn't drawing people in who had a business owner's attitude. They were people who were just looking at the value of the contracts only and weren't looking at running a business. It was either just a job or a bunch of contracts they could subcontract and make a margin on.

I was attracting low-quality candidates, not high-quality candidates who were really interested in having a sizable business or who wanted to be business owners. A lot just wanted to be cleaners earning high hourly rates. They didn't see any other value in it, and they didn't see any value particularly in paying ongoing fees. Worse because I had no track record as a franchise system and hadn't established a brand, new franchisees were bargaining and negotiating vendor finance deals with me.

One day in the first year of franchising the business, our office receptionist informed me that one of the franchisees had arrived unannounced and was filling up our office entrance with cleaning equipment – buckets, mops, vacuums, every piece of cleaning gear they had. I went out to ask what was going on. The franchisee told me calmly and nonchalantly that they weren't interested in doing this anymore and handed over all their sets of office keys. They had over $12,000 per month of accounts, and cleans had to be done that night. They had a vendor finance agreement for their franchise and treated the business as a filler job! They were just going to walk away from it.

At such late notice, my head trainer, general manager and myself were left with no other option but to go out cleaning that night.

This was not the way to run a franchise system!

To turn this around, the focus of the franchise had to be the business systems, and the support. Winning cleaning contracts for franchisees had to be the bonus not the be all and end all of the franchise.

PRO TIP

Be careful of your franchise offer.

The wrong offer will attract the wrong people.

Often what a prospective franchisee wants is different from what they need. An educational recruitment journey will also help you qualify and separate out the candidates that are right for your business.

Again, this was what I had set out to do from the beginning. The fact that we could win cleaning contracts for franchisees got their initial interest, but the right kind of franchise was interested first and foremost in having the systems and support to build a business.

To do this meant franchisees would need to be developed as business owners.

The whole franchise package had to be overhauled.

I wanted to give franchisees the training and tools to build multi-seven-figure businesses if they wanted to. This would need to encompass more than just winning cleaning contracts. It would need to include running all aspects of the business from cleaning referrals, communicating to clients, sales right up to accounts and auditing. I would attract better quality franchises doing this and attract people excited about becoming true business owners.

I hosted live workshops for franchisees, and trained them to win cleaning contracts for their own business.

In my sales workshops franchisees learnt:

- How to win profitable cleaning accounts using more than just price as the sales pitch.

- How to identify the six key factors that make up a potential client.

- The techniques that generate a constant stream of leads from direct marketing, social media, online advertising and database nurturing.

- Scripts, demos and presentations showing them exactly how to make winning proposals.

- How to follow up and close proposals.

- How to quote quickly with accurate pricing.

I provided cleaning training that covered:

- Cleaning basics. Learn methods, chemicals, cleaning hacks, and techniques as well as best-practices for safety and environmental procedures.

- Job routing and planning for maximum speed and efficiency.

- Tricks of the trade that helped them provide superior cleaning services and save massive amounts of time.

- How to surprise and delight their clients to get referrals and long-term client retention.

- Expert ways to use machinery to gain operational efficiencies for faster, better, and more profitable cleans.

Franchisees learnt how to recruit, train and manage staff. I provided them with individualized recruitment ad templates, and a guided, step-by-step recruitment process.

They learnt how to:

- Recruit cleaners who were engaged, loyal and ready to help them provide exceptional customer service.

- Train efficient cleaners who work to high standards.

- Pay staff correctly according to minimum salaries, entitlements and insurances.

- Ensure that their new team members do the little extras that make all the difference for their customers.

Franchisees mastered communication in their business.

They learnt how to:

- Communicate effectively with customers for maximum retention.
- How to use Urban Clean's innovative communication systems to differentiate themselves from the competition.
- Develop a never-ending flow of referrals.
- Put themselves in the perfect position to ask for extra jobs, upsell services or even increase their rates.

They were taught the drivers behind managing cash flow and profit in their business, such as:

- Business fundamentals, such as working capital, breakeven, and cost-management.
- How to make every client profitable.
- How to add multiple additional streams of revenue to each client.
- Ways to finance and grow your business without hurting your cash flow.
- The accounting procedures and numbers behind the business.
- How to create efficiency and profit in every job run.

In addition, I gave them full access to our systems, manuals and custom-built software, Janiflow. I gave them access to an accounts system and accounts team so they could focus on growing and developing their business, not invoicing and account reconciliation. I provided them with an integrated management system that was externally accredited to ISO 9001 standards so they could follow a world class management system in their business.

In addition, they were provided with one-on-one coaching. Regular workshops and webinars were made available to them.

To those that were more ambitious and wanted to grow a seven-figure commercial cleaning business, we created a Winners Inner Circle membership program that provided additional support and training to franchisees that wanted to grow their business fast.

The result was to attract people who first and foremost wanted to run a business. They weren't just cleaners looking for a second income. They wanted to be business owners.

Recruitment became a qualifying and selection process. The drawcard was the ability to provide cleaning contracts. But once that was combined with a sophisticated business system and training platform, I had created a powerful and nearly irresistible franchise offer.

I had created not just a franchise opportunity but a franchise system that others could duplicate. I had created a master franchise. Even if they had no background in franchise recruitment, business sales or commercial cleaning they could follow my system for recruitment and cleaning contract sales. I had people who had owned key-cutting businesses in the past and cafes with no sales background and they were able to recruit franchises and win cleaning contracts.

CHAPTER 16:
Building Residual Income

CHAPTER 16:
BUILDING RESIDUAL INCOME

"I would rather earn 1% off 100 people's efforts than 100% of my own efforts." – John D. Rockefeller

So far I've covered how to have a predictable way to rapidly win customers and keep them. This is an absolute requirement for any franchise system. I've covered how to attract, recruit and train franchisees. The last step you've got to get right is critical if you want to build a sustainable lifestyle business that enjoys residual income.

That last step is a scalable manageable system to support your franchisees.

The very first thing that you've got to get right is a selection criteria for prospective franchisees. The temptation to accept anyone with money that can fog a mirror is strong especially when you start. I can't stress enough how important it is to resist it!

Accepting poor quality candidates will always cost you in the long run – whether that's in time, money, wasted opportunity, distractions or brand damage.

Creating a list of criteria is not always easy to begin with though. It can take time, trial and error. After a few years you'll notice patterns. You'll see patterns of behavior, attributes and backgrounds that high performers share in common. Likewise you'll see similarities with low performers. There'll be subtle and nuanced things but also some things that are clear black and white indicators of future performance. If you're a prospective franchisee it's best you find out from an established and successful franchisor what these things are that they're looking for to see if you cut the mustard. If you're looking at becoming a franchisor, ideally you want a list of criteria to look for from day one.

There's a whole list of items we look at when evaluating a potential candidate. Some of the basic things we look for when recruiting a unit franchisee is their savings history, their track record of success at work and other businesses they may have owned. I'm particularly on the lookout for how they treat the recruitment team, the interactions and questions they have with existing franchisees. Do they follow through on their promises? Are they punctual? What's their understanding of basic business concepts such as cash flow, profit and working capital requirements. For instance, we don't recruit people unless we see that they've got money in the bank to cover all costs for at least the first three months of their business or they've got another income stream.

We look at their personality profile, their level of ambition and their tolerance for variety, change or stability. I want to see that they've had some roles that required supervising and customer service skills.

We have a list of specific things that allow us to say yes or no to a prospective franchisee. We want business owners after all, not cleaners.

So, you've got the right candidate, now what?

The next thing you've got to do is create online and physical reference materials, training manuals and procedures. There's a lot of work here. I'm not going to pretend that this is not an enormous task but it is absolutely critical. You have got to have these. If you are going to support new business owners, you need material they can follow so they can duplicate as close as possible a proven business system.

Also, can you imagine what it'd be like if your franchisees had to ring you up every time they had a question or a problem? This is expected to a degree when you first train and onboard a new franchisee. But there needs to be reference material they can study and go back to as they operate the business.

You've got to guide them back to reference material, step-by-step manuals and training material so they can, in a sense, follow the bouncing ball in a paint by numbers fashion. Otherwise, you're continually jumping in, telling them how to do it rather than just pointing them back to the training material and manuals that they've got 24-hour access to.

And here's the secret.

The secret is to get franchisees to take ownership and responsibility for their business as soon as possible. You do that by getting them involved from day one in their business. Even if you're winning contracts for them, get them to be part of the process. The business isn't a car that they just buy from the showroom. Buying a business and franchise is more like ordering a kit. We have the kit, the instructions and the tools. We now get to build it together with them. When people get involved from day one and see it as a partnership, people will naturally take on an 'above the line' attitude. It's simple to do but if you don't know how to do this, you're going to run into all the problems I just mentioned earlier where franchisees see the business only as a source of cleaning contracts and nothing more.

> **PRO TIP**
>
> Service fees and royalty income as a franchisor become residual income when it's easy for franchisees to operate and succeed in the business using the tools and resources available in the franchise system.

To do this, you'll need to make it easy for people to operate their business. Everything should be laid out in easy step-by-step sequences, processes and scripts. This makes support easy to provide and sustainable even with a large number of franchise partners. After training a new franchise, supporting them becomes a matter of guiding them through all support material and systems already created as a reference for them. When they have a question, you point them to the tools and resources they already have access to.

It takes time to develop but once you have it you have a one-to-many model of support. You don't want to be running around constantly, repeating yourself saying the same things one on one.

Finally you'll need a way to make sure the whole of your business is on track. Once you've set key performance indicators, standards and benchmarks, you want to measure your performance against them. This forms the basis of an integrated management system. An integrated management system is a fancy phrase that describes regular measurement and reporting of feedback on the important things of your business so you can concentrate and make changes to improve performance. Getting big is great. Getting better at the same time matters even more.

One of the best ways to see if you have a system that meets world standards is to go through the process of ISO accreditation. We did this for Urban Clean for both commercial cleaning and franchising and achieved accreditation for ISO 9001 in Quality Management, ISO 45001 in Safety Management and ISO 14001 in Environmental Management. All Urban Clean franchisees have full access to this so from day one they're operating using a world class management system that normally wouldn't be available to them until they had been in business for years and were turning over many millions of dollars. What it meant for us as a system is that we could quickly identify if improvements were needed at a local area or franchise or if system wide improvements were needed.

CHAPTER 17:
A Unique Approach to Franchising

FRANCHISE

CHAPTER 17:
A UNIQUE APPROACH TO FRANCHISING

"Work smarter not harder." – Carl Barks

Now, you might be thinking at this point, "Wow, this is way too much to expect from a franchisee of a cleaning business. How do you expect cleaners to do this sort of stuff?" But here's the thing. You're not going to recruit cleaners. If you're a franchisor you want to recruit business owners. And truth be told, people really do want to take control of their entire business. There are some commercial cleaning franchise opportunities that promise that the franchisor will take care of all the business stuff, while the franchisees just take care of the cleaning. But people that want to own a real business don't want that. When people invest in a business, they want to be shown all parts of their business including sales and management. They just need the right system, guidance and support to do that.

At this point I've shared with you the raw ingredients what's required to build a system like this. If you're looking at doing this yourself, it's going to be at least a two-to-three-year process and expect to spend at absolute bare minimum half a million dollars. And that's if you know exactly what you're doing. It cost me more and took me longer getting this thing right. Luck was on my side. Things could have turned out very differently for me. I also was fortunate to have incredible mentors and amazing people turn Urban Clean into the franchise system it is today.

The fastest way to shortcut this process and save years and perhaps even millions of dollars in development is to find a system that allows you to become a sub-franchisor or master franchisee. You can spare yourself the pain and spare yourself spending millions of dollars like I did trying to get the thing right.

PRO TIP

Work once, get paid forever should be the mantra of every business owner.

The goal of every business owner is to build a profitable commercial business that can work without them.

The right franchise gives you a massive head start in achieving this goal.

Some of the advantages of operating a master franchise like Urban Clean's is that when you recruit a franchisee you get upfront cash to scale and having staff can be optional. You can have exclusive territory rights to operate the system. You get step-by-step systems to recruit franchisees. You get a proven client acquisition system so you can win commercial cleaning contracts on demand. In your territory you have the rights to operate an entire franchise system and be a franchisor.

When I franchised the business, I realized I had something others wanted. So, we went about documenting and systemizing everything. Not just how to operate the cleaning business, but how to operate the franchise business.

I made this system available for entrepreneurs to operate in their cities and countries.

Essentially this business model is about packaging the winning of cleaning contracts into a ready-made business that has all tools for a franchisee to grow and expand and you get a percentage of everything that they earn.

This model is about doing work once and getting paid forever.

The hard work developing a system that works has already been done. Every part of the business has been turned into step-by-step procedures for you and your franchisees.

There's an intranet and manuals, where we give step-by-step processes and guides. We've laid everything out in checklists and easy to follow steps and custom-built software.

We made it simple for you to operate the business as well as your franchise partners.

There's a step-by-step process to recruit franchises. We break the process into qualifying calls, discovery, strategy and partnership sessions.

There are processes for winning cleaning contracts, very simple, powerful, predictable steps to win business. Sales scripts have been written for you.

There is a cost calculator, proposal templates and forms. To create a cleaning proposal for a prospective client you just fill their details in a form, and bang, a PDF proposal is created ready to send to your clients.

There are sales follow-up and closing sequences to follow. There are forms, templates and manuals to coach your franchisees.

Tools, manuals and resources are made available for your franchisees to operate their business.

There are sections related to operations, occupational health and safety, the administrative parts of their business, cleaning mastery, sales mastery and profit mastery.

There are simple, step-by-step guides on how to perform basic cleaning tasks, how to make sales, how to recruit, train staff and ensure they manage them, audit their cleans and obviously how to use our custom app among many other tools.

All the tools, resources, templates, step-by-step procedures that we used to build a multimillion-dollar business are made available to them.

All of this is at their fingertips and your job, as the franchisor coaching them, is to guide them through it. In your coaching sessions you'll be showing them where to find and use the tools and resources available to them so they can operate a very profitable business.

So who is going to invest in a franchise like this?

There's going to be a range of prospective franchisees looking to buy this franchise from you. Some are working during the day and are looking for a side hustle to add additional income as their own boss.

They might be wanting to buy a home, or they are looking at taking their first step into business ownership without the risk of losing their existing income. The fact you're going to set them up with cleaning contracts makes this a compelling business for them.

They don't have to quit their daytime job. They can keep it and then service cleaning contracts after hours. As they grow their business, they'll take on part-time staff. Some will quit their jobs and grow a significant sized business.

Others will be wanting to build large businesses from the get-go. They'll aim to be managing teams of staff and build a seven-figure cleaning business.

Your franchisees will be interacting with their clients themselves. That's not your role. Your role will be setting them up with some initial accounts, guiding them on how to communicate with their clients, how to do cleaning audits, and to manage their own staff and cleaning.

They manage the business at a site level. Customers love this because they get to be able to interact directly with the people in charge of the cleaning.

This is a rinse and repeat business.

You may have heard the secret to success is finding something that works and repeating it over and over again. This is one such example.

There are five simple steps.

Step 1. Recruit a franchise. A franchisee is going to invest tens of thousands of dollars with you to be set up in their business.

Step 2. Win them a set amount of guaranteed cleaning contracts.

Step 3. Win more cleaning contracts that you can sell to your franchisees.

Step 4. Earn a percentage of all the cleaning contracts you've won and that are serviced by your franchisees.

Step 5. Coach and support your franchisees to grow their business by getting new clients, increasing the dollar spend of each client, and by selling additional products and services to these clients.

Once you've recruited one franchise, you recruit another one following this exact same process. You might end up building a network of 20, 30, maybe even a couple hundred franchisees.

You make immediate money by recruiting franchises and selling cleaning contracts to them and you get the freedom and flexibility from the ongoing revenue that comes from the cleaning contracts that they manage and service.

It's the ultimate leverage. People are paying you upfront to grow your business. They manage and grow the business you win them, and pay you a percentage of their revenue.

This business model is about building solid growing, recurring income.

Staff with this model is optional. You are not responsible for cleaner salaries, supervisors or account managers. Your franchisees clean themselves, or employ, train and manage their own cleaners. They liaise and communicate with their clients.

Cash flow is not a problem when you win an account. In fact, you'll be paid money when you win accounts. And because franchisees aren't employees or subcontractors, they get paid when their clients pay them. You are not responsible for their payments. You don't need to buy machinery and cleaning equipment. Your franchisee will do that.

What this means for you is that you can get on with growing and building a business, winning more cleaning contracts without worrying that you'll grow faster than your cash flow allows. You have leverage in this business model and get to benefit from OPM and OPT – other people's money and other people's time.

Before finishing this chapter, I want to cover two popular business opportunities. If you're looking at investing in a franchise business there's a good chance you've looked at one or both of them.

The first is gyms. The good thing about gyms is that like commercial cleaning their revenue is contractual and subscription based.

That's where the advantages end. To invest, fit out and equip a gym costs hundreds of thousands of dollars.

Great locations will cost a small fortune in rent. Poor locations will turn your gym into a desert island.

Then the bills start, wages, repairs, advertising, utilities and breakage to name only some.

You need a lot of gym memberships to even cover basic costs to run the business.

And the market is saturated. It seems like there's a gym on every street corner and every shopping complex.

If gyms sound bad, they're a cakewalk compared to food franchises. They're visible. You see them everywhere and they're probably the first thing that comes to mind when you think of franchising.

It's easy to assume they're money makers. The facts say otherwise. And they're shocking.

According to a recent Franchise Business Review report 51.5% of food franchises earn profits of less than $50,000 a year. Only 7% of food franchises have profits over $250,000.

The average profit for all restaurants in the report was $82,033.

This is hardly the territory of millionaires.

This report included such big brands as McDonald's, Burger King, Dunkin' Donuts and Subway. When initial investment for a Burger King restaurant ranges from $1.8 million to $3.2 million dollars or a Dunkin' Donuts from $450K to $1.5 million, these returns for the risk you take are anemic.

If you have sales and management experience, there are much better investments that require less capital, carry less risk and promise much higher returns.

Commercial cleaning is often overlooked for these 'sexier' business opportunities. But let's compare a commercial cleaning master franchise to gyms and food franchises (See table on opposite page).

There's really no contest.

The upfront investment is typically lower.

You don't need to rent offices or have premises.

There is no equipment, maintenance, repair or refurbishment cost. Overheads are low. Staffing is optional. You can make tens of thousands of dollars from a single sale. Try selling a sandwich for that.

	Gym Franchise	Food Franchise	Unit Janitorial Franchise	Master Janitorial Franchise
Low upfront investment required	x	x	✓	✓
Home based or low rent	x	x	✓	✓
Low equipment costs	x	x	✓	✓
Low maintenance and repair costs	x	x	✓	✓
No or low refurbishment costs	x	x	✓	✓
Contractual income	✓	x	✓	✓
Recurring, residual or subscription based income	✓	x	✓	✓
Low sales skill required	x	✓	✓	x
Low employment costs and staff management	x	x	x	✓
Low stock and inventory management	✓	x	✓	✓
Opportunity to make high ticket sales	x	x	✓	✓
Low fixed overheads	x	x	✓	✓
High average profits without multiple locations	x	x	✓	✓
Can operate multimillion dollar business without employees	x	x	x	✓

Of these, the only advantage a food franchise has is that your skill level can be low to operate this business.

That is hardly a recommendation. And you will be paying a premium for it in upfront costs and ongoing overheads.

Even if your gym or restaurant made money. The returns from each location are such that you won't become rich without owning multiple locations. And if you're looking at well established brands such as McDonald's, do you seriously think the prime locations haven't already been taken?

Operating a unit franchise in commercial cleaning will mean employing staff and contractors. Your fixed overheads however are going to be nothing like a gym or a restaurant. Your revenue is recurring and made up of signed contracts. Profits can be predicted and locked in as soon as you get a new account.

A commercial cleaning business is perhaps one of the most overlooked businesses and best kept secrets in entrepreneurship.

AFTERWORD - CALL TO ACTION

"The only impossible journey is the one you never begin." – Tony Robbins

Congratulations on reading this book and learning what it takes to grow and scale a successful commercial cleaning business.

This book is your outline to financial independence with commercial cleaning and master franchising. You've read about developing a sales process for winning cleaning contracts, keeping them and using franchising as a way to fast-track results or scale your business without taking on huge risk and overheads.

I've presented two business models in this book. The first one is an operationally focused model. It is a model that allows you to build up a portfolio of clients in your spare time initially and manage client relationships and cleaning teams. You could start this without quitting your job or daytime pursuits. You don't even have to be good at sales. For those that want proven systems to follow, personal training and cleaning contracts even won for them, we developed the unit franchise opportunity.

The second business model is focused on sales and scale. It's about following a proven sales system to win cleaning contracts, recruit franchises and set them up in their business. You support but don't manage. Your unit franchisees manage their own clients and their own cleaning teams. That part of the business is theirs. Your unit franchises can of course win their own cleaning contracts, but many will want you to do that for them. You make money recruiting franchises, selling cleaning contracts to them and getting a percentage of their cleaning contract revenue. It's possible under this model to have a multimillion-dollar cleaning business without a single employee and without any of the typical overheads or liabilities associated with a business of this size.

Throughout this book, you'll notice a theme. Did you notice it?

The theme is personal freedom. Owning a successful business can be one of the most rewarding accomplishments in life. You get to provide a service people need and the opportunity to provide families with livelihoods with the jobs and opportunities you provide. But with the right business it can be something more.

Having the right business – a profitable commercial enterprise that can work without you – gives you time, money and freedom. Once you get one, you don't have to work for someone you don't like or trade your life away to pay for a meal ticket. Instead, you get to spend time with the people you love and do the things that matter most to you. You get to pursue your passions and contribute to causes that you care about. Because it's the things that happen outside of business that matter most, your personal development, your spirituality, your family and your community. Having more time and more money allows you to do more of all these things. A commercial cleaning business operated the right way can be your ticket to financial freedom.

I invite you to live your dreams. I invite you to start the next chapter of your life.

ABOUT URBAN CLEAN

The world's number 1 commercial cleaning franchise system.

This book can only be an outline and guide. It would take many volumes, how-to-guides, training sessions and workshops to go through how to do everything step by step. This book can't be a substitute for custom-built software, a set of manuals or a complete business system. If this book, though, has convinced you that a commercial cleaning business is for you, and you'd like to learn what it might look like to join forces with us and get one-on-one support with direct access to these resources I encourage you to reach out to us and discover what license or franchise opportunities are still available in your area.

Urban Clean was founded on the principle that a cleaning service could offer a consistently positive customer experience all the while providing a profitable business model for the people running and operating the business.

Urban Clean focuses on the profitable segment of the commercial cleaning market. Our service is uniquely designed to service the needs of this market with industry-only technology and systems that deliver exceptional outcomes for our clients.

Depending on your location and their availability we have Master Franchises, Unit Franchises, Licenses and Master Licenses available for qualified ambitious entrepreneurs.

Since 2014, over 180+ franchise partners have joined the Urban Clean family. After establishing a national footprint cleaning offices throughout Australia, Urban Clean has expanded internationally with opportunities now available in countries such as the United States, United Kingdom, Canada and New Zealand.

The commercial cleaning industry is huge. Billions of dollars are spent every year to keep businesses clean. A portion of those billions can be yours!

For Australian franchise information go to www.urbanclean.com.au

For U.K. franchise information go to www.urbanclean.co.uk

To learn more about U.S. and international opportunities, go to www.urbanclean.com

Or you can reach out to us directly at info@urbanclean.com.au to discuss any license or franchise opportunities that may be available.

I invite you to explore this exciting opportunity and look forward to meeting you in the future and seeing your success.

EXTRA BONUSES!!

EXTRA BONUSES HERE NOW!

We can't give you everything to get started in your business or franchise your business in one small book.

So we've created a very special website with loads of extra FREE resources, just for you.

You'll find interviews with experts, including some who were instrumental in building the Urban Clean system, covering the topics of this book.

There are checklists, reports, tips, and tools to help you start and grow your own business, invest in a franchise or become a franchisor.

Check out our Bonuses at:

www.CleanUpWithFranchising.com

ABOUT THE AUTHOR

Damien Boehm

Damien is an international author, entrepreneur and franchisor.

Damien grew up in Adelaide and overcame a challenging start to become the first member in the history of his family to finish a university degree. After completing his degree, Damien traveled to Korea and Indonesia to teach English. He then returned to Australia and built, sold, and developed millions of dollars' worth of property in his twenties before discovering a lucrative business opportunity.

Damien is the founder and CEO of Urban Clean, a national commercial and office cleaning franchise. Started as a side business in 2009, Damien franchised the business in 2014. It now has more than 150 franchisees across Australia and is expanding internationally.

Urban Clean is a member of the Franchise Council of Australia. It generates millions of dollars in annual revenue and its strategic business model helps its franchisees to build scalable, profitable businesses.

Damien attracted the interest of renowned international business entrepreneur and founder of ActionCOACH Brad Sugars to partner with him to further develop his franchise and take the concept global. Urban Clean has serviced thousands of clients and cleans some of the biggest companies in Australia.

About the Author

In addition to working in Korea and Indonesia in his early twenties, Damien has traveled extensively to further his personal and professional achievements. Countries such as USA, the UK, Germany, the United Arab Emirates, China, Taiwan, Japan, South Korea, Malaysia, Indonesia, Fiji and New Zealand.

Damien is an avid pilot with a passion for planes, books, traveling and bike riding.

Damien is the author of *'Clean Up with Franchising'* and lives in Brisbane with his wife and their three children.

Ingram Content Group Australia Pty Ltd
Printed in Australia
AUHW011017010623
378998AU00014B/14